Loving and Leaving

LOVING
AND
LEAVING

Winning at the Business of Divorce

by

BERNARD ROTHMAN, J.D.

Lexington Books

D.C. Heath and Company • Lexington, Massachusetts • Toronto

A GENE BUSNAR PRODUCTION

Library of Congress Cataloging-in-Publication Data

Rothman, Bernard.
Loving and leaving : winning at the business of divorce / by
Bernard Rothman.
p.   cm.
Includes index.
ISBN 0-669-20944-9 (alk. paper)
1. Divorce—Law and legislation—United States—Popular works.
2. Divorce—Economic aspects—Popular works.   3. Divorce—
Psychological aspects—Popular works.   I. Title.
KF535.Z9R645   1990
346.7301'66—dc20
[347.306166]   90-6216
CIP

Published simultaneously in Canada
Printed in the United States of America
Casebound International Standard Book Number: 0-669-20944-9
Library of Congress Catalog Card Number: 90–6216

The paper used in this publication meets the minimum requirements of
American National Standard for Information Sciences—Permanence
of Paper for Printed Library Materials, ANSI Z39.48-1984.

Year and number of this printing:

91 92 93 94 95 8 7 6 5 4 3 2 1

To my wife, Barbara S. Rothman.

"I am to my beloved as my beloved is to me"

From the Song of Songs.

*To our children, Brian, Adam, and Helene, their spouses
Vicki and Suzanne, and our grandchildren, Seth and Joshua.*

*To our parents, Rebecca and Harry Rothman and
Edythe and Samuel Schaeffer.*

Contents

Acknowledgments

I WOULD first like to thank my friend and partner, Allen Finkelstein, Esq. He has been a bulwark of support throughout this project.

Thanks also to my buddy and partner, Stuart Abrams, Esq., with whom I have practiced law for almost two decades. Stuart has participated with me in the real-life drama that forms the basis of the case histories described in this book.

I wish to acknowledge the efforts of my daughter, Helene Rothman, a student at Hofstra Law School, who was my research assistant in this project.

Special thanks to Dr. Norman J. Levy, an extraordinarily gifted psychoanalyst and one of the most supportive and caring people I have ever met.

Much of the material contained in chapter 10, "Leaving Home," was taken from an article that was coauthored by Dr. Paul Nasser, Andrew Schepard, Esq., and myself, and was published in the New York State Bar Association's *Family Law Review* of September 1987. The article was stimulated by a conference on the same subject with the same title and format that was organized and presented by the Interdisciplinary Forum on Mental Health and Family Law.

The Interdisciplinary Forum is a working group of appointed liaison representatives from legal and mental health organizations concerned with promoting discussions between the respective professions on family-law-related topics. The conference was the first time the legal and mental health professions exchanged ideas on the leaving-home problem in a formal academic setting in the New York City area. Some of the material contained in the article had its origins in what transpired at the conference. I thank the members of the Interdisciplinary Forum and my copresenters at the conference: Rona Shays, Esq., program moderator; Paul Birzon, Esq.; Hillell Bodek, C.S.W.; Sandra Jacobson, Esq.; Kenneth Kemper, Esq.; Dr. Ruth Ochroch; and Dr. Paul Nasser.

A note of thanks must go to Rona Shays, Esq., with whom I have had the privilege of cochairing the Interdisciplinary Forum of Mental Health and Family Law since its founding in 1986. Rona has been a tireless and selfless advocate of the cause of interdisciplinary cooperation.

The work of the Interdisciplinary Forum was made possible by the enlightened leadership of recent presidents of the New York Chapter of the American Academy of Matrimonial Lawyers, to wit, Paul Birzon, Esq., Sanford Dranoff, Esq., and Alvin Ashley, Esq. Sandy Dranoff, the incoming national president of the Academy, has pledged to continue to advance and strengthen the cause of interdisciplinary cooperation on a national level.

I am grateful to those who specifically contributed to the writing and publishing of this book. Gene Busnar, an exceptional collaborative writer, has been a source of inspiration, insight, patience, and sensitivity. His untiring efforts have contributed immensely to bringing this project to fruition.

Thanks also to Dr. Naomi Leiter, Dr. Sylvan Schaffer, Julian Block, Esq., and Andrew Shepard, Esq., for their contributions to this book. Thanks to Jeff Herman, literary agent extraordinaire, and to Jamie Forbes for his efforts in transcribing and editing portions of the manuscript. A deep bow to Sandra Jacobson, Esq. for her careful and insightful review of the book. My work would have been more difficult without the efforts, understanding, and dedication of my secretary, Mary Casale. A vote of appreciation to my sons, Brian and Adam, who acted as a sounding board for me.

Finally, to my wife Barbara who has been, as always, a source of love, comfort, guidance, patience, balance, and inspiration throughout this project—thanks for everything!

Author's Note

M ANY of the case histories and anecdotes in this book are based on my professional experiences. Others are fictional or based on composites. All names, places, and specific details have been changed to protect the confidentiality of the people involved.

Although many friends and colleagues have assisted in reviewing the text of this book, the author assumes sole responsibility in the event of error.

Loving and Leaving

1

Can You Win at Divorce?

THE breakup of a marriage is one of the most devastating emotional experiences a person can face. And while divorce is not always the best solution to marital problems, one out of every two married couples in America will go that route at least once.

When I first meet new divorce clients, I always ask them if anything can be done to preserve the marriage. In some cases, I suggest counseling or psychotherapy as a more appropriate and less costly alternative to divorce—particularly when there are children involved. Unfortunately, by the time many people consult an attorney, it is too late for reparative measures.

Social scientists have pointed to divorce as a phenomenon that may ultimately jeopardize the very fabric of our lives. Unfortunately, they have been unable to offer any long-term solutions to the problems that underlie broken marriages. As an attorney who practices primarily in the marital area, I am on the front lines of the divorce wars every day. Though I must admit that I also have no easy answers for lowering the divorce rate, I can help you avoid the kinds of expensive financial and emotional mistakes so many others have made in the past.

People often talk about winning at divorce in terms of property splits or custody settlements. After twenty years of handling divorce cases, however, I have concluded that the only real winners are those who can get on with their lives unencumbered by hatred, guilt, or the need for retribution. To do that, one has to approach the whole process with some understanding of the legal, financial, and emotional issues that come into play.

My purpose in writing this book is to give you the information you need to make appropriate and positive decisions— whether you are in the midst of a divorce, contemplating a breakup, or thinking about formulating a premarital agreement with your prospective spouse. Before I explore specific aspects of the delicate business of loving and leaving, I'd like to give you an overview of the complex mix of factors that come into play so that you'll be better able to chart your course. Let me begin with a piece of basic but essential advice.

Take Control—Stay Rational

Since divorce unleashes some of our most highly charged emotions, it is easy to become overwhelmed. Nevertheless, your ability to assume control and to take positive action under difficult circumstances can be the most important factor in how well you survive a divorce. Your attorney will be there to negotiate on your behalf and to provide counsel and support along the way. Keep in mind, however, that the ultimate responsibility for making intelligent and appropriate decisions lies squarely on your shoulders.

No matter where you are in the divorce process, it is crucial to proceed in a rational manner. Doing otherwise can result in wasting thousands of dollars in unnecessary legal fees. Worse still, you can bring about a negative emotional climate that will haunt you long after the legal aspects of the divorce are finalized. Let me give you an example.

I represented a wealthy dentist who had been married for twenty-seven years. As part of the divorce settlement, the couple's home was to be sold, with the wife receiving part of the proceeds. The wife was required to move by a certain date, but she refused to do so—despite the pleas of her children and her attorney. My client decided to stand on principle. He insisted that his wife be held in contempt for her failure to comply with the court order.

At my client's request, I obtained a second court order holding the wife in contempt, but she still stubbornly refused to move. The husband continued to insist that his wife vacate the premises, even though the house was still not under contract to be sold and there really was no reason—other than spite—to force her to leave. Nevertheless, my client insisted that I obtain an order of arrest, which I did.

Three days later, his wife was arrested and brought into court in handcuffs. This caused my client to break down and sob uncontrollably. The judge directed the wife to vacate the house immediately or face a jail term for contempt of court. At that point, she moved.

My client later told me that for many months afterward he would often wake up in the middle of the night in a cold sweat, shaken from a nightmare in which he saw his former wife standing before the judge in handcuffs. This man had gotten his victory, but at what price?

When a marriage ends, emotions tend to run amok. For, whatever else it may be, divorce represents the disintegration of some of our most highly charged dreams. Let's look at how easily these dreams can degenerate into nightmares.

We Americans are a particularly dream-oriented people. We have our dream house, our dream car, and our dream job. But in no area of life is the dream more intense—and yet more potentially harmful—than in our pursuit of love and marriage.

Far too often, our idealized dreams contain little or no understanding of ourselves, our mates, our interpersonal relationships, or the obligations and realities of marriage itself. We simply dream, and hope that our marriage will last forever—without growth, without introspection, and without pain.

A man may dream that his wife will be a mother-figure, a fashion plate, a friend, a meticulous homemaker, or a sex goddess. A woman may dream that her husband will be a provider, a jock, a hunk, a devoted father, or a strong protector. Many of us enter marriage with fantastic visions of earth-shattering, climactic sexual performances that will last forever—despite economic problems, job tensions, and the stresses of family living.

Couples who reflect too little and pursue the dream as if it were reality are likely to become embroiled in disagreements over money, family responsibilities, children, and personal freedom. The longer mutual problem solving is delayed or avoided, the greater the sense of frustration, anger, and boredom becomes.

In time, positive communication may completely disappear. At that point both spouses experience a profound feeling of failure, which they often convert into an attack on the other as a means of preserving their sense of adequacy. When married couples become adversaries, the war over their economic survival and emotional identity can escalate rapidly. Finally, there is one overriding emotion: revenge at any price.

I represented a successful businessman in a particularly bitter divorce proceeding. This man derived a substantial portion of his earnings from cash transactions that were not declared as taxable income. His wife, an M.B.A., who worked as an executive in a major advertising company, knew about his income tax cheating. In her quest for vindication, she decided that the best way to "nail the jerk" was to report him to the Internal Revenue Service for tax fraud.

The wife's attorney tried his best to persuade her not to do so. Among other things, she had signed joint income tax returns with her husband and, therefore, would not qualify as an innocent spouse. Unfortunately, her lawyer was unable to convince her that this spiteful course of action was likely to backfire.

The tax people investigated and assessed some fifty thousand dollars in taxes and penalties for which husband and wife were jointly responsible. In the interim, my client suffered a business reversal and filed for bankruptcy. He became bereft of assets and income. Unfortunately for his wife, she was financially solvent.

Now, Uncle Sam will take payment from whichever party has the money, regardless of the apparent equity of the situation. Thus, the wife—not the husband—was required to pay the full fifty thousand dollars in tax assessments, plus fines, penalties, and interest.

The estranged couple's volatile emotions are but one part of a perplexing situation. The divorce nightmare operates concurrently in a number of areas—all of which have an adverse effect on one another. The emotional battle between husband and wife is complicated by at least three other major factors: the adversarial nature of attorneys, the inevitable delays of the courts, and the ambiguity of divorce law.

The Attorney's Role in the Divorce Process

People sometimes ask me if lawyers are the only real winners in divorce cases. Since attorneys are generally compensated for their services on an hourly basis, they do stand to make more money when cases drag on. By that same line of reasoning, people may also feel that physicians are the only real winners when patients require extended treatment for cancer, heart disease, or other serious illnesses.

In law—as in medicine—there are good and bad practitioners. As a consumer of these critical and expensive services, you owe it to yourself to be highly selective and choose professionals you can trust. To get maximum value for the dollars you spend on legal fees, it is important that you understand something about how marital lawyers operate.

Divorce proceedings take place within the framework of an adversarial legal system in which each side tends to be more concerned with victory than justice. There is no denying that we of the matrimonial bar are a litigious breed. No matter how honorable our intentions might be, we sometimes find ourselves caught up in the heat of battle. It is extremely difficult not to react when you feel that your adversary is trying to pull a fast one. The unfortunate part is that when lawyers become embroiled in a game of one-upmanship, it is the clients who foot the tab.

Attorneys have an obligation to make certain that their egos do not stand in the way of resolving a case. However, that's not always easy. I don't think there is any experienced lawyer who has not, on occasion, had to wonder: "Am I doing this because it's in the client's best interests, or am I doing it because of my personal need to beat my adversary?"

The other side of the coin is that attorneys have to be careful not to personalize the client's fight and make it their own. When a client hungers for vengeance, the last thing he or she wants is a lawyer who talks in terms of negotiating in good faith and shaping an equitable divorce settlement. As a result, attorneys are often placed in the rather strange position of having to prove that they are tougher and meaner than their adversaries. (In that regard, I recently saw a T-shirt with a logo that read: "My lawyer can beat up your lawyer.")

One key to avoiding these escalating adversarial problems lies in your selection of an attorney and the kind of relationship you establish. It is important to find someone whose attitude and temperament reflect your own. Since your attorney works for you, he or she, within the bounds of professional ethics and judgment, should act in accordance with your wishes. Always ask yourself where your best interests lie: do you want to wage a full-scale war, or would you like to resolve the situation in an equitable manner and get on with your life?

I've seen more than a few cases in which a husband or wife will spend thousands of dollars in legal fees arguing over the possession of ashtrays, cups, and other items that could be purchased for next to nothing. Attorneys are responsible for making clients aware that such action is ill-advised. Nevertheless, it is important to keep in mind that your lawyer does not have the last word in what transpires—you do!

Our Cumbersome Legal System

The couple's explosive emotions and the brinksmanship of their attorneys can make matters difficult enough. But this complex situation is further exacerbated by the ponderous nature of our court system. Trial delay is one of the few immutable principles of the divorce process. Fewer than 10 percent of matrimonial cases are tried to a decision by the courts. The real action takes place out of court—in *motion practice* and in financial *discovery* before trial and in negotiation between the attorneys.

If a settlement cannot be reached by the spouses and their attorneys, the case will eventually go to court. As soon as a trial judge enters the picture, you have absolutely no control over how your case ultimately will be resolved. You can be sure, how-

See the glossary for definitions of italicized terms.

ever, that things will proceed at a snail's pace. Unless you are a lawyer or judge, you may not be aware that courtroom procedures do not correspond to the same logic as the rest of the world.

Let's assume, for example, that you are trying to establish the value of real estate. In order to do so, you must offer expert testimony as to the value. Your attorney would be obliged to follow formal and time-consuming rules of evidence. Here are just a few of the questions an attorney might ask to qualify the appraiser as an expert:

- How long have you been a real estate appraiser?
- Approximately how many houses have you appraised in this area?
- Did your appraisal assignments include residential and commercial real estate?
- Did your appraisal assignments include improved and unimproved real property?
- Have you testified before in court as an expert in the field of real property valuation?
- How many times?
- Do you belong to any professional societies and organizations?
- Have you had any writings published in the field of real estate appraisal?
- What type of information did you collect to aid in this appraisal?
- Is your fee in any manner contingent upon your testimony or the outcome of this case?

After taking perhaps a half-hour to establish the appraiser's expertise, the attorney finally would be able to ask the five-second question: What is the fair market value of the house? If the other attorney objects to some of the questions, it can take an entire morning to qualify that real estate appraiser as an expert.

Similarly, in some divorce cases, you can go through the same cumbersome process trying to establish the value of every piece of marital property. If there are substantial assets to be divided, you may have to drag into court twenty experts and subject them to the same lengthy process. Of course, while all this is going on, you are paying your attorney by the hour.

Changing Laws in a Changing Society

Additional time and legal fees are not the only problems you face when your divorce reaches a courtroom. As I mentioned earlier, the interpretation of many divorce laws is currently in a state of flux. Therefore, when you proceed to trial, you often have little ability to predict what the outcome will be. This is particularly true when shifting social values or unconventional mores are brought into play.

I recently represented a woman who had divorced her husband to live with a man who is bisexual. My client very much wanted custody of her two children. Under more usual circumstances, the mother probably would have little difficulty obtaining custody. However, there is no telling how a judge might respond to the question of whether this unusual living arrangement would provide a suitable environment for children. In the end, a judge's strong personal (often unarticulated) feelings may play a greater role than somewhat ambiguous legal precedents.

When you consider the unfortunate mix of emotional, financial, and legal issues involved in a divorce, you begin to understand the importance of formulating what I call a rational plan for winning. In subsequent chapters, I will show you how to develop such a plan so that you can protect yourself every step of the way. But before you even consider initiating legal action, I suggest that you take stock of your emotions and personal feelings. Perhaps divorce is not the real answer to your problems. Too many people hire attorneys to vent emotions that could be dealt with more effectively in psychotherapy or marriage counseling.

Let me give you a poignant example. I recall a case involving a sixty-three-year-old retired New York City schoolteacher in a divorce action that was initiated by her husband, a sixty-five-year-old former salesman. Shortly before the couple was married, the wife had inherited a great deal of money. Suddenly, after twenty years of marriage, the husband decided to leave. It seemed to me that this man was having Walter Mitty fantasies that caused him to act impulsively. One day he apparently had decided he had to change his life before it was too late. So, he picked himself up and just walked out of the marriage. What made this man's motives even more questionable was his belief that he would be entitled to half of his wife's inherited money as part of the divorce settlement. I felt that the wife had a strong case for not giving him one red cent.

In New York—as in forty other states—marital property is divided under the principle of *equitable distribution.* In essence, this means that all property acquired during the marriage is considered part of the financial settlement upon divorce. However, property acquired by a spouse before the marriage or by inheritance is not generally considered part of the marital pot, unless there is a specific *prenuptial agreement* that provides for the division of such property.

Since no such agreement existed in this case, I felt that a judge would rule that the wife's inheritance was her separate property and, therefore, not part of the settlement. That is exactly what happened. This misguided husband was not awarded any of his wife's money upon divorce. Today, he is poorer and more unhappy than when he was married.

Many people divorce for inappropriate reasons or on impulse. As you progress in your reading and become more knowledgeable, you may ultimately decide that it would be in your best interest to reconcile with your spouse. If, on the other hand, you conclude that it is too late for reparative measures, I will show you how to negotiate the steps of divorce with a minimum of financial expense, legal complications, and emotional bitterness.

Whatever your decision, your actions must be supported by a willingness to assess the situation objectively and to accept responsibility. I believe that if you start with a take-charge attitude and use the information and strategies contained in this book, you will maximize your chances of emerging from the divorce a winner.

2

Can Planning for Divorce Save Your Marriage?

I F we were sitting face-to-face, I'd try to find out all about you, so I could start dealing directly with your needs.

Perhaps you'd tell me that you're about to get married, and want to sign a *prenuptial agreement*. Perhaps you're married and want to have more control over financial and legal matters. Some of you may be thinking about divorce—or maybe your partner has already made that decision for you and is saying: "Speak to me through my lawyer."

Wherever you are in this process, there are certain basics you'll need to know.

In chapter 1, I discussed your need to emerge from this process a winner. An important first step in that direction is understanding the relevant issues so that you can start taking appropriate action. Another key to winning at this game is recognizing how much control you have over your destiny.

Men and women in the throes of divorce often feel helpless and unable to control their circumstances. But no matter how it may appear—even in the darkest, most uncertain hours—you can weather the storm. One of the main reasons I wrote this book is to give you a place to turn for help. Some of you will be able to get many of the answers you need from these chapters. Others will need the more intensive, personalized advice of a good attorney and/or mental health professional.

Fortunately, there is a great deal of legal and emotional help available. Still, it's you who must shoulder most of the responsibility for moving ahead with your life. Attorneys and therapists can only help to guide people through the maze of legal, financial, and emotional issues that are part-and-parcel of the divorce process. The client must, however, take charge. When you retain one or more of these skilled, highly paid professionals, remember that in the final analysis they are your employees. You are the boss! Let me tell you what I tell my clients:

"If you want to use my knowledge to your advantage, you must recognize that even the best attorney is nothing more than a skilled navigator. Ultimately, you are the captain of your ship."

The earlier you assume a take-charge attitude, the better your chances are of coming out ahead—legally, financially, and emotionally. If you don't take control, you turn the decision-making process over to others by default. That also is your choice—but one that can be extremely costly.

In the final analysis, attorneys and therapists have only as much power as you give them. That's why it's so important for you to understand the relevant issues and learn to make informed choices. With this in mind, I'd like to start unraveling things. Let's explore some basics that will enhance your understanding, wherever you happen to be on the marriage–divorce continuum.

The Making and Breaking of a Delicate Partnership

Maybe you've never thought about it in this light, but the moment two people marry, they form a financial partnership. For many of you, this will represent the most important business commitment you will ever make.

I've often thought about how helpful it would be if the clergyman or judge told us that when we take those marriage vows we are also entering a business relationship. Unfortunately, too many couples just plunge into marriage with no real discussion or understanding of these matters.

When one of the partners makes a unilateral decision to get out of a marriage, it becomes extremely difficult to approach a settlement with a cool head. No matter how hard you try to keep the discussion centered on financial issues, you can never totally prevent all sorts of highly charged emotions from entering into the mix.

If you're going to stay afloat in such potentially treacherous waters, you must learn to deal with complicated and often volatile feelings. No matter how intense your emotions run, you owe it to yourself to stay rational and to maintain control of the situation. Otherwise, it's going to be impossible to move forward in your life—much less win.

In recent years, more and more couples are facing the realities of the future breakup of their unique partnership by setting up their own marriage contracts. These contracts are called *prenuptial* or *antenuptial agreements* when they're signed prior to the marriage. When such contracts are signed after a couple is married, they are called *postnuptial agreements.*

WHAT CAN BE COVERED IN MARITAL AGREEMENTS?

In general, marital agreements can cover a wide variety of issues. They can define what is *separate property* and what is *marital property.* They can address issues such as *maintenance, spousal support,* and *child custody,* including such issues as education and religious training of children. The agreement often also covers asset distribution upon death.

Basically, as long as there has been full and honest financial disclosure by each spouse, the courts will uphold virtually any provision of a prenuptial or postnuptial agreement as long as it was entered into voluntarily and in good faith and it was fair and reasonable at the time of signing the agreement and not unconscionable when the agreement is enforced. Generally, however, provisions relating to custody, care, and maintenance of children are not binding on the courts.

Before I discuss some of the particulars of executing and enforcing these agreements, let me attempt to answer the question I'm most often asked concerning marital contracts.

Do I Need a Prenuptial or Postnuptial Agreement?

The thinking on this issue is split pretty much down the middle. On the negative side, one can argue that when a couple starts dividing assets even before taking their vows, they've created an emotional climate that can have destructive consequences.

Picture the setting: You're holding your lover in your arms. He just pledged his undying love, and suddenly, in the next breath, he says: "Honey, in case our marriage doesn't work out, I'd like to protect the assets I've worked so hard to accumulate. If it's okay with you, my lawyer will call your lawyer in the morning."

Not a very romantic scenario, is it? Such a proposal is hardly likely to fuel the fires of passion or generate a great deal of trust. After all, who wants to work out the terms of a divorce before they're even married?

Yet we come back to the sobering reality that, whatever else it may be, marriage is a legal and financial partnership. Most informed women and men would not even consider entering into a conventional business relationship without drawing up some kind of contract. Why, then, should the partnership of marriage require any less protection?

Since the business of marriage is one that also involves our most profound emotions—not to mention those of our families—one can argue that it makes sense to take whatever protective measures are readily available.

One out of every two first marriages in the United States will end in divorce. That's why there's something to be said for accepting and understanding this very real possibility early on in the game. Setting up a prenuptial or postnuptial agreement serves four major purposes:

1. Initially, it spells out the terms and protects your financial interests in the marriage.

2. If at some point divorce appears to be the only alternative, a prenegotiated marital agreement can put you in a position of greater strength and minimize your financial hardships.

3. It allows you to determine the distribution of your estate.
4. It may save the children from becoming pawns in the divorce war.

I talked earlier about the dangers of entering a marriage solely on the basis of dreams. Sure, romantic love and sexual chemistry are important components in any relationship, but marriage also involves any number of practical realities. Whether or not you decide to draw up a formal marital agreement, it's a good idea to have some open discussions about finances and child-oriented issues early on. When you initiate a frank and open dialogue with your partner, you create a climate of mutuality and joint decision making that can have a positive long-term effect on the marriage.

As I see it, money is a language between married people—just as sex is a language. If two people can start communicating openly and honestly about difficult issues, they will greatly improve the quality of their relationship.

Unfortunately, even the most open communication can't guarantee a lasting marriage. Still, if your marriage ultimately doesn't survive, the chances for an equitable, mutually acceptable divorce settlement are far greater when the financial split is negotiated in advance. Divorcing couples who don't execute a marital agreement must hammer out a financial settlement in accordance with state laws.

A *community property* system applies in ten Western states. The courts in those states divide marital property equally upon divorce. However, property acquired before marriage or by gift from the other spouse or by inheritance is not subject to division. The vast majority of states now have an *equitable distribution* system. This means that on divorce all *marital property* should be split fairly and equitably, though not necessarily equally, between the spouses.

In essence, all property acquired jointly or by either spouse during the marriage is considered part of the marital pot to be divided upon divorce. Not all states agree, however, on what constitutes marital property. In some states, property acquired by one spouse before marriage (*separate property*) is not part of the marital pot. In other states, premarital property is not recognized as such, and forms part of the pot. In many equitable distribution states, gifts from one spouse to the other are not marital property, while in a minority of states interspousal gifts are considered marital property.

Furthermore, the equitable distribution laws also take into consideration a variety of factors in determining how the marital pot is divided upon divorce, such as the length of the marriage; the age, health, and earning potential of each spouse; the amount of spousal support to be received; and the tax consequences of such transfers. This uncertainty is one reason why the vast majority of divorce cases never actually go to trial. Most people feel (quite correctly) that they have more control if their divorce can be settled through out-of-court negotiations.

It's important to recognize from the outset that these dealings are always much more contentious—and costly—when couples perceive the negotiations as a war over their emotional and economic survival or over their children. That's why there's a lot to be said for working out a split of the marital pot and child-care arrangements while the relationship is still solid.

At this point, you may perceive that I'm recommending that every couple turn to their attorneys and have a prenuptial or postnuptial agreement drawn up. Actually, that's not the case. Basically, my position is balanced between the two extremes. I believe that every couple should understand, at the very least, the financial consequences of entering a marriage—as well as the ramifications of terminating the relationship.

The majority of couples who marry for the first time probably don't need to have a formal marriage agreement—especially if there are only a few sizable assets involved at the time of the marriage. In fact, such couples may be better off without one. Couples with modest assets might find it disruptive to start anticipating financial inequities that may or may not come into play five or ten years down the road.

Of course, you can always draw up a postnuptial agreement. But at that point, you have to ask yourself if such a measure is really necessary and appropriate. It might not be very comfortable, however, after ten years of marriage, to ask your spouse to sign a postnuptial contract—without a very good reason.

Actually, I find that many couples who draw up prenuptial agreements often tear them up once they're convinced of the permanence of the relationship—usually after about ten years. In some cases, there is a *sunset provision* written into the contract causing the agreement to become null and void after a specified period of time.

Before you decide whether a prenuptial or postnuptial agreement is right for you, let's explore the four general instances in which formal marriage contracts are most appropriate:

1. One of the spouses is entering the first marriage with far more assets than the other.
2. One or both of the spouses has already gone through a divorce.
3. One or both of the spouses has children from a previous marriage.
4. There has been an aberration in the marriage, which has been righted.

1. Rich Spouse/Poor Spouse—First Time Around. Let's look at a hypothetical young couple about to marry for the first time. She's a secretary and he's a junior vice president and owner of a small piece of a lucrative family-owned business. The couple is very much in love. There is an implicit sense of trust between them—and financial problems are the furthest thing from their minds.

Not surprisingly, the groom's parents don't share their son's carefree attitude. They want to be sure that in the event of a divorce their future daughter-in-law will not try to lay claim to a piece of the family business. While this is a valid concern, it can put pressure on a young couple and create a climate of distrust. If the groom seeks a prenuptial agreement because of his parents' wishes, the young bride may feel that the groom's parents don't approve of the marriage. Perhaps she may perceive they think she's a gold digger who's marrying primarily for the money.

In such a situation, it's understandable for the groom's parents to harbor such thoughts, even if they insist that their desire for a prenuptial agreement is nothing more than a prudent business measure. After all, there are other family members involved here. Why should this outsider be allowed to pose a potential threat to the financial future of so many people?

It is my feeling that, on balance, a prenuptial agreement is appropriate in this case. But it must be approached very delicately. In the course of dealing with the financial realities, an all-out effort must be made to preserve the quality of the young couple's emotional relationship. This is not easy to accomplish, but with mutual respect and understanding of both counsel and the parties, it can be done.

At some point, every married couple must deal with differences and problems. Most people choose to postpone the inevitable, and that's perfectly understandable. But our hypothetical couple is facing an issue that requires them to remove their rose-colored glasses sooner rather than later.

In this case, the groom's family is asking the couple to take a worst-case approach. This is not going to be very pleasant. Still, if it's handled correctly, it can result in some very positive long-term benefits.

In fact, a prenuptial agreement can actually serve some of the same purposes as premarriage counseling, because both generate a frank dialogue between couples about the realities and potential difficulties that are part-and-parcel of the impending marriage. One would hope that the bride can be convinced that this is not a personal affront to her character by her future in-laws—and by extension, by their son. If the bride feels she is being unduly pressured or forced to sign an agreement, it can put a cloud over the marriage for years to come. Instead of letting negotiations sour a couple's feelings, prospective spouses can use them as an opportunity to develop skills for resolving differences and building a stronger marriage.

2. Second (Third or Fourth) Time Around. There's a line in an old Frank Sinatra song: "Love is lovelier the second time around." Far be it from me to argue with such a deliciously romantic sentiment, but to my mind the real question is: Can people who've been through the mill of a bitterly contested divorce enter a new marriage with anything close to the same sense of starry-eyed optimism they brought to their first marriage? I think not.

Human nature being what it is, there's bound to be a feeling of mature reservation and prudent distrust when one or both of the spouses has been divorced. There are understandable concerns by those who've been through the mill. They're likely to be awakened at 2:00 A.M. by a little voice asking: "Are you sure you're doing the right thing?"

People who marry for the second or third time have had more time to accumulate assets—either from work, from a divorce, or from an inheritance. For example, a divorced woman may be collecting *maintenance* from her ex-husband. Since these payments normally terminate upon remarriage, she may want written assurance that, if the new marriage ends, maintenance payments would resume, courtesy of her new husband.

Since people in such circumstances frequently have more to protect and more to lose on divorce—as well as stronger concerns that things may eventually fall apart—they have a greater need for the kind of comfort and security a marital agreement provides.

3. Children from a Previous Marriage. People entering into a second or third marriage often have children from the previous relationship(s). This can make matters far more complicated. Men and women in this situation often feel that whatever assets or estate was accumulated during the previous marriage should belong to their children upon their death. A *prenuptial agreement* can give them that protection.

It's not hard to understand why someone entering into a second marriage wouldn't want their new spouse's children sharing in an estate they have worked long and hard to build. Many people also don't want the new spouse to have any part of assets that accumulated during the previous marriage. This is also quite understandable. Men and women in this category can execute prenuptial agreements that specifically address those concerns. At the same time, they can deal with any number of related questions that might arise.

What if the newly married couple buys a house taken in the husband's name, with money that was accumulated by the husband before the marriage? How will increases in the value of the husband's *separate property* be handled? What if the title is taken in the name of both spouses? Does the husband consider that a gift to his spouse?

Here again, the best solutions are forged when husband and wife work together to resolve things in an equitable manner. But as the issues and solutions become more complex, so does the need for a written document spelling out the terms of the financial partnership.

Despite the complexities involved in negotiating the financial particulars of a second or third marriage when either or both spouses have children, it is possible to hammer out an arrangement that is satisfactory and equitable to all concerned.

4. An Aberration Has Taken Place. Let's assume that a marriage of ten years was going relatively smoothly. All of a sudden, the husband falls in love with a much younger woman and leaves home. Divorce proceedings are initiated by the wife. Each spouse retains counsel, and negotiations begin.

Six months later, the husband realizes he made a big mistake, and begs his wife to take him back. She's willing to reconcile. But, understandably, she's far more skeptical about the prospects for this marriage than she was before all this happened. Under the circumstances, she would be well-advised to require a *postnuptial agreement* as part of the reconciliation.

People who have gone through some of the angst of divorce can never again view marriage with as much optimism as they once had. This kind of aberration in a marriage can be rectified, but it certainly gives you an appreciation of how important it is to protect yourself, particularly if you are the spouse on the receiving end. Still, no matter who causes the aberration, both parties should proceed cautiously in repairing a damaged relationship.

I recently represented a husband who was seeking a divorce. The couple had been married for seven years and had a four-year-old daughter. The husband was a principal in a family-owned dress-manufacturing business.

The couple had been separated for about a year, and the husband was living in a rented apartment. Both spouses were dealing with issues in a reasonable manner. My settlement negotiations with the wife's attorney were proceeding fairly smoothly. There were just some minor items to iron out before final settlement. Suddenly, my client called and said that all bets were off.

My client had been on an overseas business trip for the past month, and while he was sitting in a hotel room in Hong Kong, he started rethinking the wisdom of his going through with the divorce. As he continued to reflect about how empty life would be without his wife and daughter, he realized that he was about to make a terrible mistake.

Immediately upon returning from abroad, he called me to announce that he and his wife had decided to give the marriage another try. Within a week, he moved back into the family home. Naturally, I was happy to hear the good news. I'm a family man myself, so I could appreciate his joy. But as so often happens in such cases, I had to temper my enthusiasm with a few words of caution.

My client had been in the process of buying more stock in the family business. He and his brother were also thinking about expanding into some new business ventures. I felt obliged to warn him that until he was at least reasonably certain that the marriage was ultimately going to work out, he should not buy any more stock in the company or expand into any new business ventures.

My client protested that these business maneuvers he contemplated would have substantial short- and long-range tax benefits, as well as enormous profit potential. Nevertheless, I had to counsel him that such moves were ill-advised. I bluntly told him that, from an economic point of view, he could be compromising his position.

I was concerned about what would happen if he proceeded with his plans, and if, six months later, the marriage fell apart again. He would have acquired some new, very substantial assets that would be considered *marital property* in the event of a divorce.

Before the aberration in this marriage occurred, there was no marriage contract. At the time, that seemed perfectly appropriate. But now that the couple had gone through the preliminary steps of a divorce, things would have to be viewed in a different light—at least for a while.

If my client had determined to acquire the new assets, it

would have been foolhardy for him not to insist on a *postnuptial agreement* designating the new assets as his *separate property*. At the same time, requiring a postnuptial agreement at this tenuous point in the relationship might have undermined the couple's chances of working things out.

As it developed, my client took my advice and held off expanding his business interest for one year. At that point, both spouses felt far more comfortable about negotiating a postnuptial agreement that protected both of their interests.

Terminating a Marital Agreement

When the husband and wife in the above case signed their postnuptial agreement, they requested a *sunset provision* to take effect after ten years. It was felt by all concerned that this was more than enough time to repair any bonds that may have been broken, and to restore a feeling of mutual trust and good faith between the spouses.

For couples who sign prenuptial agreements, ten years later is also the time when many couples choose to tear up the contract. However, some couples terminate the contract in five years, others in seven—whatever feels comfortable. You can set an arbitrary date and ask your attorney to write it into the agreement, or you can simply decide to declare it null and void at any time by mutual consent, so long as it is done in writing and in conformance with the laws of your state.

For most couples, the most pressing concerns are at the very beginning of the marriage, when economic inequality exists between the spouses. However, at some point in the relationship, many couples feel that their emotional commitment to one another obviates the need for the protection of a formal contract. Early on in the marriage, it's important not to let emotions prevent you from recognizing that you've entered into a complex economic partnership. But once you've made it through five or seven years together, you're likely to be well past the transitional stage. Most importantly, however, before termination of an agreement both partners should understand the whole package of legal, financial, and emotional issues with which they are dealing.

Altering a Marital Agreement

Many of the pressing issues that make a *prenuptial agreement* initially desirable are likely to change as the years go by. Once children enter the picture, a host of new considerations emerge. Even though you and your spouse are financial partners, are you really going to renegotiate and update your prenuptial agreement every time a new child is born? I can tell you from experience that very few couples take this approach.

Of course, there can also be many financial changes that alter the economic balance in a marriage. The secretary who married into a wealthy family seven years ago may have gotten her M.B.A. and a high-paying job. At the same time, the husband's family business may have gone bankrupt, and he now may be making less money than his wife. Should this couple alter their prenuptial agreement?

Again, if the marriage is viable, most couples tend to dispense with, rather than alter, an existing prenuptial agreement. Of course, the choice rests with you and your spouse. If you do amend, you must repeat the same formalities, and, most importantly, you must update financially. What if the two of you can't agree on the terms of revision? Where would you go at that point? You'd either have to sit with the original agreement or void it and take your chances—except now you've created an adversarial situation that surely can't help the marriage.

Every attorney has his or her own feelings and personal preferences about the issue of marital contracts. Some disdain prenuptial agreements—except in rare cases. Others will tell you that even the poorest couple can't afford to be without one. As I said before, my position lies between these two extremes. When couples are acting out of knowledge and in good faith, it's always possible to find a solution. The important thing is that you've considered the relevant issues and that you're both comfortable with the arrangement.

Legal Requirements of Marital Agreements

I mentioned previously that marital agreements can address a raft of issues, including the division of assets, the length and amount of *alimony* or *maintenance, child custody,* and the disposition of the estate. In any event, however, an agreement should adhere to the following guidelines:

- The agreement must be fair, reasonable, and not unconscionable—both upon signing the agreement and at the time of its enforcement.
- Both parties would be well-advised to have separate legal counsel.
- The agreement must be in writing, and comply with any other technical requirements of your state.
- Most importantly, there must be complete and honest financial disclosure by each party.

Let's look at the meaning and impact of some of these important guidelines.

While the laws in most states allow couples a great deal of latitude in structuring their marital agreements, the parameters of the agreement have to be reasonable and not unconscionable to either party. Thus, if there is any hint of fraud or deception in the making of the agreement, a judge may declare any relevant provision—or the entire document—null and void.

Technically, it's possible in many states for a couple to retain one attorney to draw the agreement. However, I strongly advise that each party retain separate counsel so that there's no question about each party having been completely and independently apprised of all the relevant facts. Once divorce proceedings begin, it's easy for one spouse to claim that he or she was deceived by the other. I've seen it happen more times than I'd care to remember. "We went to my husband's lawyer," one wife protested. "He wasn't looking out for my interests, so I really didn't know what I was signing." This is a familiar refrain, and one that can call an entire marital agreement into question.

Once a couple makes a decision to have a marital agreement, they should treat it like any other business decision. What if you were negotiating a business partnership agreement or a stockholder's agreement with a close friend? Wouldn't it go without saying that you'd each retain separate counsel? That is also the only rational way to set up any kind of marital contract—at least if you want it to be enforceable.

The concepts of reasonable and not unconscionable can get a little tricky, but certain aspects are quite cut-and-dried. Obviously, if either spouse can prove fraud on the part of the other, the court may declare some of or the entire agreement null and void. That's why it's absolutely essential that each spouse present a complete and honest financial disclosure of all assets. That means everything, without exception!

Marital agreements can also be set aside if duress or deception can be proven. This brings to mind the case of a seventy-six-year-old man named Ira and a twenty-eight-year-old woman named Nan. Before they met, Ira had been married twice, and Nan had been married once.

Ira was in the Bahamas on an extended vacation trip when he met Nan, who was visiting there for a one-week winter vacation. The couple had a whirlwind courtship and were married two weeks later.

Nan wanted to sign a prenuptial agreement, but the marriage took place so quickly that they decided to have a postnuptial agreement instead, and they used Nan's attorney. Nan insisted upon and Ira agreed to give Nan four hundred thousand dollars in bonds no matter what else took place if they divorced. The bonds represented Ira's total assets. Two weeks after they were married, the couple signed the agreement.

A few days later, Ira left on a short trip to visit an ailing relative. When he arrived back at Nan's house, he found the locks changed. He could not convince Nan to let him into the house, and Nan told him in no uncertain terms that the relationship was over. "Goodbye to you and the horse you rode in on," she said, without embarrassment. "I will now get the four hundred grand, sucker. You're no longer welcome in my house, so you can just get out of here!"

This case is still in litigation. Nan is alleging that she is entitled to the bonds, come what may. There's a reasonable chance the agreement will be thrown out because the court is likely to hold that it is unconscionable and accept Ira's contention that the only reason Nan married him was to get her hands on his money.

This is the kind of situation that is feared by many people who have sizable assets. That is why there is often a provision in a marital agreement that the couple must stay together for a minimum number of years before the nonmonied spouse can lay claim to any assets of the monied spouse. Even such precautions, however, don't always provide an ironclad shield as protection from dishonorable intentions.

Sometimes the problem with a prenuptial or postnuptial agreement rests not in the intentions of the parties, but in the changes that take place between the time the agreement is signed and the time it is sought to be enforced. Economic or other circumstances in a couple's life can alter conditions that would cause a judge to refuse to enforce an existing agreement.

Let me give you an example—one that's not nearly as far-fetched as you may think. In fact, it happens all the time. Phil and Ellen get married, both for the second time. He's fifty, she's forty-five. Both have children. He has substantial assets—more assets than she has. They enter into a prenuptial agreement with a provision that his assets remain his *separate property*.

In the event that Phil dies first, Ellen will get twenty-five thousand dollars from his life insurance policy. She will have no claim on the rest of his estate, all of which will go to his children. Ellen also waives all *maintenance* in the event of a divorce. Instead, she agrees to accept a relatively modest lump sum, which will increase depending on the length of the marriage. Whether or not Ellen made the greatest deal for herself is open to question. Nevertheless, these are the parameters the spouses and their attorneys think are appropriate at the time.

The couple is happily married for five years. Then tragedy strikes. Phil has a massive heart attack and needs triple-bypass surgery. For the next five years, he is unable to work. Instead of putting Phil into a nursing home, Ellen quits her high-paying job in order to care for him at home. Phil makes it clear that her personal care will speed his recovery.

Ellen's attorney urges her to alter the existing prenuptial agreement. Under these unforeseen circumstances, she certainly seems entitled to be compensated for the substantial sacrifices she is making on her ailing husband's behalf.

For whatever reason, Phil keeps stalling. "Everything is going to be okay in a few months," he tells her. "Then we can talk about revising the agreement." Unfortunately, Phil dies quite suddenly—with the original prenuptial agreement intact.

Under the circumstances, some judges might refuse to enforce the original agreement if Ellen chose to contest it. Why? Because even though the conditions of the agreement were fair and reasonable at the time of its execution, they were unconscionable at the time of its enforcement. The agreement had become so unfair that no right-thinking person fully apprised of his or her rights would ever sign it if they knew what the conditions would be at the time it was to be enforced.

In connection with enforcement of marital agreements, as in many aspects of family law, there are few clear-cut answers. That's why it's essential that you understand the many complex issues that come into play. In the final analysis, planning for divorce may not save your marriage. Then again, it may. But, at the very least, by understanding what's involved, you can attempt to structure the basis for a more amicable and equitable divorce—one that makes it easier for you to steer your life in a more positive direction.

3

Protective Measures and Rational Steps

W HETHER or not you and your spouse draw up a marital agreement, I strongly advise you to start taking the partnership aspect of your marriage seriously—no matter where you are on the marriage–divorce continuum. The sooner you start looking at your marriage as the economic partnership it is, the better off you will be. This goes for wives as well as for husbands—nonmonied as well as monied spouses. Let's take a moment to examine some contrasts.

Women vs. Men/Monied vs. Nonmonied Spouses

Back in the old days, the working husband traditionally entered a marriage with more assets than the nonworking wife. Though the balance has certainly changed over the past few decades, certain generalizations remain with respect to financial dealings between spouses.

In the old-fashioned, stereotypical household, the husband was the primary breadwinner, while the wife's role was to take care of the home and children. Despite societal changes, there are still many marriages in which the nonworking wife is completely unaware of what's going on financially. Such an approach is ill-advised.

Both spouses should be aware of the implications of the family-partnership concept. The wife who hasn't paid attention to family finances should, for her own benefit, become much more involved and aware. Let me put it even more bluntly: It's foolhardy for any woman not to know how much money her husband is earning and what the family assets are.

In interpreting the *equitable distribution* laws, the courts in the majority of states are giving more and more recognition to the homemaker's financial stake in the economic partnership of marriage. This has important implications for both spouses.

Even if a wife (or nonmonied spouse) doesn't want to take a particularly active role in the economic management of her family, she should at least make certain that her participation in this partnership is acknowledged by her spouse and protected by prudent action.

At the same time, the husband (or breadwinner) in a one-income family has to recognize that any business decisions he makes also involve his wife. If, for example, he expands his pre-marital business and the value of that business increases, the wife will most often be entitled to a portion of that appreciated asset in the event of a divorce. This is true whether or not the wife had any knowledge of the expansion—or even if the husband conducted the entire transaction from a bank account that was in his name only.

The courts in most states are making it abundantly clear that they intend to uphold the principle that marriage is a true economic partnership. Does this mean that all assets will be split fifty-fifty in the event of a divorce? Not necessarily. At least not yet. Still, every married person who wants to protect his or her financial interests needs to be aware that most economic choices can have a potential impact on a divorce settlement. That should be reason enough to start getting your financial affairs in order. But there are other considerations as well.

From an emotional standpoint, it makes good sense for both husband and wife to take an active part in the management of their economic affairs. Mental health professionals with whom I have spoken have concluded that couples are less likely to divorce when both partners share in making economic decisions.

When both spouses participate in the management of their economic partnership, many subtle advantages accrue. If open discussions and joint decision making take place early in the game, the whole fiber of the relationship can be strengthened.

I find that when both partners are involved, there is a better distribution of responsibility all around. This kind of give-and-take tends to keep the emotional balance in a marriage on a more even keel.

While it is essential for both partners to take an active role in financial matters, I have seen more wives than husbands make the mistake of being passive in these matters. That's why I think being aware of the financial ramifications of marriage and divorce is particularly important for women, who traditionally have come out on the short end of the financial stick in divorces. Nevertheless, there are signs that the scales have started to shift in recent years.

In evaluating the financial terms of a divorce, judges are now more likely to consider such factors as a wife's efforts in maintaining a household or working to help her husband obtain a professional degree or to build a business. This has resulted in a somewhat more equitable division for women. Nevertheless, the wife's share of total marital assets often still averages 30 to 40 percent or so.

Estranged wives suffer other inequities as well. Only 15 percent of divorced women have ever been awarded *alimony*. Furthermore, women with children have been awarded sufficient money for child support in only 50 percent of divorce cases.

Despite a gender bias in our system that apparently favors men, the majority of divorces in the United States are initiated by women. In fact, Census Bureau statistics show the typical demographic of a person most likely to initiate a divorce to be an urban-dwelling woman in her thirties who has been married for less than five years.

There has been much written and said about the inequities that women suffer in a divorce, and I certainly would not dispute that generalization. Nevertheless, it seems to me that the pendulum is starting to swing more in women's favor.

There certainly have been a number of court decisions that are inequitable to women. It's also true that the vast majority of domestic relations judges are men—which may predispose them to empathize with the husband's position. Nevertheless, many of the claims that say women invariably get the short end of the stick are based on only a small percentage of cases.

Remember, nine out of ten divorce cases are settled out of court between the parties and their attorneys, and the terms of those settlements don't necessarily favor the husband. At least that doesn't seem to be the feeling among the attorneys I know. Please don't misunderstand. I'm not saying that the system is free of sexism—far from it. Nevertheless, I believe there is reason for optimism.

In recent years, there has been pressure on many state legislatures to include in the concept of *equitable distribution* the presumption of equal distribution—unless the court has specific reason for ruling otherwise. This trend toward a true fifty-fifty split is one that bodes well for women.

While the debate about sexual bias and equal property division in the divorce process is not likely to subside any time soon, I believe that members of both sexes have much to gain by taking the kind of protective measures I am about to outline. If you feel especially vulnerable—whether man or woman—your best defense may be a good offense.

What it comes down to is a question of choices. Are you willing to take a clear-headed look at issues as they present themselves, or will you insist on waiting until things reach the crisis stage?

There was once a popular television advertisement for a well-known motor oil. The thrust of the ad was that drivers who changed the oil in their engines every three thousand miles could avoid major car-repair bills. As the mechanic stood there holding up a can of motor oil, one driver pulled his energetic car out of the station. Meanwhile, a second driver shook his head in despair at his car being towed into the service bay for major repairs. The mechanic eyed both cars. "You can see me now," he said, looking at the healthy car that just received its regular three-thousand mile oil change. "Or," he shook his head sadly, motioning toward the broken-down car, "you can see me later."

It seems to me that a similar principle applies in winning at the business of divorce. You can choose to take a few relatively easy steps early on that will help protect you from more serious problems. Or, you can wait until your marriage has fallen apart, and those once-simple steps have been transformed into over-whelming complexities. The choice is yours.

Suggestions to Help You Start Taking Control of Your Financial Partnership

Right about now, I'll bet many of you would like to ask: "What are some simple preventive measures I can take to help protect my rights?"

As discussed in chapter 2, drawing up a *prenuptial* or *postnuptial agreement* is a good idea for some couples. Let me now outline four other protective measures that I am comfortable suggesting across the board. All of these are inexpensive and easy to implement on your own to help you start taking control of your financial partnership:

1. Take an active role in your family's finances. It is essential that you and your spouse have candid, open discussions about your financial relationship. By doing so early on, you can greatly improve the communication between you and your mate.

2. Don't ever sign a tax return or other financial document without reading and understanding it. If you don't understand what you're reading, consult an accountant or attorney.

3. Initiate a full economic disclosure as soon as possible. Be apprised of all your income, stocks, pensions, insurance policies, real and personal property, your debts, and how you spend your money.

4. Keep financial records. Know all bank account numbers; have keys to all safe-deposit boxes; retain a copy of all legal and financial documents.

I feel that the first three suggestions I have listed are fairly self-explanatory. In chapter 5, I will get into the particulars of what's involved in a complete financial disclosure. For now, I'd like to discuss an extremely important preventive measure—one that seems to inspire a great deal of resistance in many people.

The Importance of Good Record Keeping

As with so many other steps that go into winning, keeping complete and accurate financial records is helpful in good times—and a shield against possible disaster in bad times. Most people don't derive a great deal of pleasure from diligent record-keeping. Still, if you're willing to devote a little time to it on a regular basis, you can do yourself a great deal of good.

I realize that it's impossible to keep every single bill and scrap of paper forever, yet it's prudent to keep important documents in a safe place, so they can be retrieved if they're ever needed. I also recommend keeping some kind of annual financial diary. There are small booklets available at commercial stationery stores for this purpose, or you can devise your own. In either case, it's actually not that complicated. People who are in business often keep a running diary of their activities so that they can present some documentation to the Internal Revenue Service (IRS) about deductions being taken in case of a tax audit. Now, most people are never audited. So why, you may ask, should one bother keeping a diary?

Let me respond by asking a few more questions: What would happen if you were audited? How would you prove to the IRS that your business deductions were valid? Do you think it's likely that an auditor would simply take your word without any substantiation?

Since the chances of divorce are far greater than those of being audited, common sense dictates that one exercise at least as much prudence. That's why I think it's a good idea to maintain a running financial diary that contains some basic financial data and a history of what takes place each year.

Such a book might include the following kinds of information:

- Name(s) of employers
- Wages, commissions, royalties
- Major purchases—and how they were financed
- Gifts

- Inheritances
- Stock purchases and transfers
- Vacations
- Itemized living expenses for the family
- Insurance costs
- Loans

In addition to making specific financial entries, it's also a good idea to note any significant events that occurred in a particular year. If, for example, your spouse took a two-month leave of absence from work because of illness, write that down. If that required you to work more hours to compensate for the financial loss, put that down as well. Some things may seem too minor or petty to enter, but if there's any doubt in your mind, put it down in your running diary. Basically, I would include everything that in any way relates to your financial relationship.

In the event of divorce, a running diary will help you and your attorney ascertain your contribution to the marriage—which may greatly strengthen your position when it's time to cut up the marital pie. Please understand that a running diary may not be enough to establish absolute proof of your position. As with a tax audit, you may be required to produce receipts, bank records, and other contemporaneous documentation.

The reality is that over 90 percent of divorce cases never go to trial, but are instead settled by negotiations between the attorneys. It's always a great benefit when your adversary feels that you have enough documentation and evidence on your side to prevail in court. That's one good reason why record-keeping is so important.

If your marriage is currently relatively solid, you may feel uncomfortable about planning for the worst. Indeed, many people don't draw up a will or obtain life insurance because they fear that it will, somehow, turn into a self-fulfilling prophecy.

In a less dramatic way, it can also be distressing to think, for example, about keeping records of whether inherited monies were used to buy stock or a house. Still, details like these can have a major impact when it's time to divide the marital pie.

As I will discuss more fully in chapter 5, money obtained by one of the spouses through inheritance is generally considered to be *separate property* by the courts in about half of the *equitable distribution* states. Once that money is commingled with joint funds, however, it transmutes from separate (or nondistributable) property into *marital property* that is subject to distribution.

An enormous amount of time, money, and effort goes into the preparation of a divorce action when attorneys and accountants have to gather financial records to establish the parties' financial contributions to the marriage. To distribute the assets of a marital partnership equitably, one needs to know exactly what each party brought into the marriage, and what each subsequently contributed. I've run into case after case in which one or both of the parties are unable to substantiate their relative financial positions. This makes it very difficult to engage in meaningful negotiation.

The need for substantiation becomes even more acute if the case goes to trial. Among many other factors, a judge needs to know what the spouses' economic positions were, both at the beginning of the marriage and at the time the divorce action started. How else will the judge be able to determine what constitutes an equitable split of the marital pie? If you go into court unable to document your contribution to the partnership, you surrender a great deal of control over your destiny and expose yourself to a lot of unnecessary risk.

I remember one case in which the wife claimed that the ten thousand dollars used as the down payment for the family's house was a loan from her mother to the newly wedded couple. The husband, on the other hand, claimed that the money was a gift—not a loan.

Unfortunately for the wife, there were no records to support her contention that a debt was still owed to her mother. The mother couldn't find—or never had—anything to document that an outstanding loan existed. No bank records could be obtained to substantiate the transaction. Finally, the attorney who handled the closing for the parties had died in the interim, and his records were irretrievable.

After a good deal of time and expense, nothing that would substantiate either of the parties' claims turned up, and we were all back to square one. If this case ever went before a judge, it would come down to a question of *testimonial proof*. In that instance, it would be up to a judge to believe or not believe what was being said. And obviously, it's not wise to leave that to chance.

So what is the message here? Certainly, I'm not suggesting that you keep every scrap of paper and receipt that passes through your life. Let's face it: You're not going to spend the bulk of your time documenting every penny you spend and everything you do. Still, it's important that you take some basic protective steps in your marriage. This is all part of taking a rational and reasonable approach to the contingencies in your life.

Let's look at another example. Most people have some kind of comprehensive theft-and-fire insurance on their homes. But if your property was stolen or destroyed, would you be able to prove its value to the satisfaction of your insurance company's claims department?

Let's assume that you have fire insurance on your apartment in the amount of thirty-five thousand dollars. A fire destroys everything. You go to the insurance company and say, "My place was gutted. Pay me thirty-five thousand dollars for the contents." You can bet that the insurance company is going to turn to you and say, "Just a minute, where are your receipts?"

All you can do is sit there with your face hanging and say, "But I don't have any receipts for this stuff. I never keep any receipts. That's just not the way I live my life."

At this point, the claims adjuster is going to look at you and say, "Tough cookies, Charlie. I don't accept your statement that you had a couch in the living room worth five thousand dollars. It's up to you to show me something that will establish its value."

I realize that most families aren't going to pay an appraiser thousands of dollars to establish the value of their possessions. Still, there are some inexpensive but meaningful measures you can take. For example, you can take color photographs of every room in the house and put them in a safe-deposit box, along with any other important documentation. At least this would show the kind of furniture you have in the house, and an insurance company would have to give that some credence.

So we come back to the concept of taking protective steps to insulate yourself from the what-ifs of life: tax audits, destructive fires, sickness, death, divorce—none of this stuff is pleasant to think about. But it's far worse dealing with these negative eventualities if you've done nothing to prepare for them.

As you're finding out, many of the positive, protective steps that you can take while your marriage is still viable aren't so very different from those you will be forced to take in the event of a contested divorce. But at that point, the emotional climate and the financial costs will be radically different.

Instead of taking care of business while things are nice and calm, you'll be trying to establish your economic position in the heat of battle. In the final analysis, it's like what our friend in the motor oil commercial said about taking care of your car: You can do it now or you can do it later. Remember, the choice is yours.

4

Choosing the
Right Attorney

When Is the Right Time to Hire a
Marital Attorney?

Unless you and your spouse intend to draw up a marital agreement, there is no need to consult an attorney on a preventive basis. As soon as you sense that your marriage may be heading toward a breakup, however, you should consult an attorney who is experienced in family law. Obviously, if you have evidence that your spouse has been cheating, or if he or she has moved out—even temporarily—consultation is imperative.

On the other hand, you—rather than your spouse—may be the one who is moving to end the marriage. Perhaps you've broached the idea of seeking counseling, but your spouse has been unresponsive. If so, it might also be a good idea to consult an attorney.

Seeing a lawyer doesn't mean that you're definitely heading for a divorce. An initial consultation, however, can make you aware of your options and give you a head start in answering the following important questions:

- What grounds for divorce do I or my spouse have?
- What percentage of marital assets am I likely to receive or have to pay?

- What assets would be included in the distribution?
- What will happen to the marital home/apartment?
- How would my present life-style be affected?
- How complicated and expensive is a divorce action likely to be?
- How much maintenance would I receive or pay, and for how long?
- What would be the legal ramifications of a trial separation?
- Who is likely to be awarded custody of the children?
- How much child support would I pay or receive?
- What would be the arrangements about life or medical/hospitalization insurance?
- Are there any measures I can take to protect myself—without exacerbating the situation?

I must caution you that even the best attorney cannot glibly answer these questions with any degree of certainty, since there are probably going to be far too many variables involved. Nevertheless, I think it's fair to say that an experienced practitioner should be able to give you an overall sense of your prospects. These projections, to a great extent, would be based on the attorney's experience and his or her familiarity with how the laws of your state are being interpreted.

In talking about initiating a divorce, it's important to be aware of the differences between the rejector (the spouse who is initiating the proceeding) and the rejectee (the spouse who is on the receiving end). There are many obvious and subtle differences in how people in these contrasting positions respond. These differences may affect how and when someone selects an attorney, as well the way many other factors are handled throughout the divorce process.

Think about it. If you're the spouse who is initiating the divorce, you have—at least in theory—a great deal more control. It is you who decides when to act and when to let your spouse know about your intended actions. Nevertheless, there are some potential dangers for a rejector.

As the spouse who is initiating the divorce, you may feel a tremendous sense of guilt and regret. I have seen many clients riddled with these feelings because they're breaking up the family unit. It some cases, their guilt may be well-founded.

It's not an attorney's place to counsel clients in the mental health area—except, perhaps, to suggest that they seek psychological help before making a final decision. But remember, even the best counselor or psychoanalyst can only advise and help you steer your ship. In the end, only you can make the really important decisions in your life. And the decision to divorce is a particularly gut-wrenching one—especially when children are involved. You can expect to go through months—even years—of anguish before the plus side of the equation starts to emerge. But this is the price we must sometimes pay to move ahead in our lives.

For the rejectee, the initial anguish is generally more intense. Yet, in a way, the choices are simpler. Someone else—your spouse—has made the decision that he or she wants a divorce. Perhaps this is only a temporary aberration and things can still be patched up. On the other hand, the die might already be cast and a permanent split might be unavoidable.

The first thing a rejected spouse has to do is to recover from the initial shock of this devastating trauma. I've consulted with many rejected husbands and wives who've told me that they were thinking about ending the marriage but never could bring themselves to do it. Then suddenly, the decision was taken out of their hands; divorce was thrust upon them like some enormous tidal wave—with a feeling that can be very much akin to drowning.

When I meet someone in this predicament, I stress how important it is to seize control of the situation. Consulting with an attorney can be an important first step in that direction because it allows you to start evaluating your life in rational terms. And this ties in with the long-range goal of emerging a winner.

Studies have shown that divorce is the second most devastating experience a human being can encounter. Only the death of a loved one is worse. I'm sure you've heard the expression: "Look for the light at the end of the tunnel." I find this to be a helpful way to view divorce and other crisis situations. As difficult as divorce is, it's often the best alternative in an imperfect world.

In a very real sense, the upheaval of a divorce can provide you with an opportunity to assert your newfound independence and permit you to start taking control of your life. Part of the emotional upheaval people go through involves letting go of the familiar and facing the unknown. While I am a strong proponent of marriage, I've seen too many people remain in bad relationships simply because they were afraid to let go of a familiar arrangement. In order to move ahead in our lives, we must have the courage to leave familiar but destructive situations that we use as comfort zones. Staying in a bad marriage can, in some instances, be compared to drug abuse. We know it's doing us harm, but we've come to depend on it.

If you are the one initiating the divorce, you may feel overwhelmed by guilt and remorse. If you are the person being rejected, you may feel helpless because everything seems to be happening outside of your control. Either way, this may turn out to be a golden opportunity for you to reevaluate and reconstruct your life.

As you proceed through a divorce, I want you to try to use that experience to enhance your self-esteem. The process of finding a good marital attorney can be a step in the right direction, if you approach it correctly.

How to Select the Right Marital Attorney

Finding a good lawyer isn't comparable to selecting a husband or wife. On the other hand, your choice of legal counsel also can have a lasting impact on your future life.

The first rule in finding a professional to help you navigate the legal waters is to seek out lawyers who have experience in marital cases. In most states, there is no specific certification or specialty recognition for attorneys who handle family law cases or any other type of cases. Thus, in New York, for example, an attorney cannot represent that he or she is a "specialist" in any area of legal practice. Nonetheless, the person you're looking for should be someone who devotes most of his or her working hours to the area of family law.

Most families have an attorney for handling real estate closings, wills, accident cases, and the like. If one or both of the spouses are in business, they probably engage other attorneys to handle those matters. As competent or helpful as these professionals may have been in the past, let me tell you why it's often inappropriate to use them in a divorce action—unless you have the simplest uncontested matter, with little property to divide, and no custody issues. There are so many legal and financial issues that go into a divorce action that generally, only someone who deals with such cases on a regular basis is likely to have the experience to be cognizant of all the factors that can potentially help or hurt your position. Also, the way the courts interpret the laws is in a constant state of flux. An attorney who doesn't regularly practice in the family law area might fall seriously behind in terms of vital knowledge.

Few other legal areas involve as many complexities as does a matrimonial action. A real estate closing, for example, is almost pro forma by comparison. The attorney examines the contract, makes sure that everything is in order, and advises the client on that basis.

The attorney negotiating a business deal also has a far easier row to hoe. In the majority of business dealings, the client knows what the parameters are. Generally speaking, the lawyer's primary job is to draw up the documents. While it's true that complex and lengthy negotiations are sometimes involved, they are rarely conducted in the kind of tempestuous emotional climate you're likely to find in a divorce proceeding.

For better or worse, the attorney's role in a matrimonial case is far more delicate and complex than in virtually any other area of the law. People in the throes of divorce are experiencing an intense personal crisis. That's why clients often require an extraordinary amount of personal attention from their attorneys. In most other contexts, clients rarely have day-to-day contact with counsel. But in a matrimonial case, it's not unusual for clients to be on the telephone with their attorneys day after day.

As you know, the termination of a marriage is about much

more than legalities and finances. For most people, there are huge emotional overtones to the entire process: You're anxious; you're concerned; you feel guilty; you feel like a failure; you're fearful about the future. When there are children involved, the fears and potential problems can escalate geometrically.

The right attorney is someone with whom you can discuss these problems on a continuing basis—someone with whom you feel comfortable. As you go through this difficult process, you will need more than just a competent professional to be your advocate. You will want to feel that you have a friend who will help steer you through difficulties.

Not every attorney is comfortable operating in such an emotional climate. In fact, many of my colleagues in the legal profession go out of their way to avoid this kind of work. Like many of my colleagues who have devoted a substantial portion of their professional lives to this field, I feel this kind of work is a calling. I like helping people sort out their lives and watching them move ahead. I get as much satisfaction seeing clients rise above the emotional turmoil as I do when I help them achieve a fabulous financial settlement.

I'm not saying that there's any one profile to look for in a good marital attorney. I just want to encourage you to find someone who is in this field by choice—not by default. When you interview attorneys, ask them what percentage of their practice is devoted to marital work. As a general rule, you should try to find an attorney who devotes at least 50 percent of his or her practice to such cases. You may want to ask each lawyer you interview how many contested divorce cases he or she has handled in the past year. If the answer is less than ten or fifteen, that may indicate that marital work is just a sideline.

It's also a good idea to find out the attorney's competence in trial work. Even though it's unlikely that your case will ever go to trial, it's essential that the opposing attorney perceive your counsel as someone who is fully prepared and willing to go to court if things can't be resolved through negotiation.

In your search for an attorney, you are likely to come across several qualified marital practitioners. Even though you may be experiencing some intense emotions, you should relax and try to get the most out of your search for the right attorney.

Although there are a number of special considerations involved in selecting an attorney, you will have to use the same kind of common sense and gut feelings you would employ in your selection of any professional whose services you require. Let me give you some guidelines for making your choice:

What to Look for in a Marital Attorney

1. PROFESSIONAL QUALIFICATIONS

I've explained why it's important to find someone who is experienced in marital work and current in the laws of your state. But there are some other qualifications to look for. Perhaps the attorney in question has published articles or books or lectures in the marital field. This would indicate that he or she has a strong professional interest in questions of family law. You might also inquire whether the attorney takes an active role in the marital section of the local, state, or national bar associations.

2. GOOD COMMUNICATION AND EMPATHY

You and your attorney are likely to be working closely together for some time to come, so you want to have a good feeling about the person—as well as a sense that he or she understands and empathizes with your situation. It's hard to know just how much stock to put into a first impression, but it often pays to trust your gut feelings.

If the attorney you're interviewing is someone you can't relate to on a human level, there are likely to be some serious problems down the road. That's why you should ask yourself if this is someone you like—and who seems to like you.

One of the questions that often arises is whether the gender of an attorney is important. Some women feel that a male attorney might not be able to be as supportive as a female attorney. Other female clients have told me that they were hesitant to work with a female attorney because they feared she might be overpowered by a male adversary.

Frankly, I don't feel that a person's gender should be an issue in your selection of an attorney. Over the years, I've seen an equal number of good, bad, and mediocre practitioners of both sexes. Nevertheless, if some people have a predisposition to work with an attorney of a particular gender, I have no problem with that. Human nature being what it is, when someone feels strongly that they will be more comfortable with a man—or a woman—it probably will work out that way.

Far more important than finding an attorney of a particular sex is finding one with whom you can communicate. If you're not asking the right questions or revealing key facts, it's up to your attorney to obtain them from you.

As your case progresses, you will want your attorney to explain what's going on in plain English. Since the vast majority of you are not attorneys, there are certain complexities that may be particularly difficult to follow. Nevertheless, you have a right to an explanation whenever you require one. And in case your attorney hasn't read this book, don't be afraid to remind him or her who is the captain of the ship and whose job it is to navigate.

3. OBJECTIVITY AND TOUGHNESS

While it's important to work with someone you like—and who likes you—I don't think you should get too carried away with the issue of good vibes.

Don't select a lawyer just because he or she tells you what you want to hear. The last thing you want is someone who routinely assures you that you're in a great position instead of cautioning you about serious issues and problems that are likely to arise. Believe me, it's far better to choose someone who will be frank about what lies ahead.

An attorney's objectivity during an initial interview can tip you off to his or her temperament and general approach. Remember, there will be times in the weeks and months to come when you'll need your lawyer to take a tough stance. That's why you don't want to retain a lawyer who is too reticent or wishy-washy about telling you what may lie ahead.

4. ETHICS AND FAIR BUSINESS PRACTICES

When an attorney is anything less than completely forthcoming and candid in assessing your situation, it may give you reason to question his or her motives. Even under the best of circumstances, a contested divorce is likely to be a costly affair. That's why you want to make sure that you're getting your money's worth.

It is difficult for attorneys to estimate with any accuracy what the total fees will be in a hotly contested divorce action. There are simply too many unknowns involved. Still, you have a right to expect an experienced practitioner to outline some very general parameters.

Since most attorneys charge by the hour, the fees on any given case will be greater when things drag on. It's improper for an attorney to give you a false picture of what lies ahead just to get you as a client.

I believe that the great majority of my colleagues are honest. Still, I know there are exceptions. That's why I want to caution you to avoid practitioners who you suspect are anything less than completely ethical.

5. FEES AND DISBURSEMENTS

When you meet with an attorney for the first time, find out how he or she charges. At this writing, an attorney's hourly fee can vary from one hundred and fifty dollars an hour to four hundred dollars an hour or more—depending on the state and the practitioner's experience, reputation, and the difficulty of your case.

Once you select an attorney, he or she will probably ask you to sign a *retainer* agreement. In retaining an attorney's services, you will probably be asked to pay in advance for the first ten to fifteen hours of his or her time. If, for example, an attorney plans to bill you at two hundred and fifty dollars an hour, he or she may ask you for a retainer of three to five thousand dollars.

Two issues that new clients frequently ask about are travel and telephone time. In the course of handling your case, your attorney may have to travel to court or to the office of your spouse's attorney. Generally speaking, you will be billed for the attorney's travel time. The reason for this is that the attorney, at least in theory, could be billing that time for work on another aspect of your or some other client's case.

You can also expect to be billed for time spent on the phone with your attorney. Make sure you're aware of how this is being handled. Some firms charge for a minimum of fifteen minutes of time, even if the length of the call is far less. In that instance, it would be prudent to save your questions until you can make full use of that minimum.

In addition to an attorney's hourly fee, you will also be charged for *disbursements*. These may include messengers, photocopying, fax expenses, secretarial overtime, and the like. A fair-minded attorney will try to keep these and all costs down to a minimum.

If legal research is required for your case, the attorney may be able to have that done by a *paralegal* and bill you at a lower fee. If some of the legal work is being done by an associate attorney, make sure that work is being billed at that attorney's fee, which also may be lower.

If you will be required to retain the services of an expert witness—such as an appraiser, accountant, private investigator, actuary, or mental health specialist—you will be responsible to pay for those fees.

New clients are often wary of how much good attorneys charge. I would be the last person to deny that these services are expensive. The more experienced and more reputable the attorney you choose, the more his or her time is likely to cost.

If you feel that one attorney's fee structure is too high, you can often find someone who will charge less. But in making that decision, you have to evaluate what's at stake and just what you're going to get for your money.

If there are not a lot of assets involved, if there are no children, and if neither partner is asking for *maintenance*, then perhaps you do not need to hire one of the more experienced lawyers in town. But if the stakes are high, and especially if your spouse has hired someone who is very experienced and reputable, a particular attorney's somewhat higher fee may not be a very significant consideration in the long run.

In any case, you should read the *retainer* agreement carefully before you sign. Be sure to question anything you don't understand, and don't be shy about trying to negotiate any terms that seem less than reasonable.

6. AVAILABILITY

One frequent complaint about attorneys is that they're difficult to reach on the phone. Think about it: If an attorney were really interested in running up your bill, why wouldn't he or she answer every single phone call, spend unlimited time talking, and indulge each client's need for catharsis and emotional support?

On balance, an attorney should be reasonably available to speak to a client, but there have to be certain limits. I am often busy with a critical matter, when suddenly my secretary announces that Mr. Jones is on the phone. Since I'm relatively sure that he is calling to ask about a document that I haven't yet received, I will tell my secretary to inform him of that piece of information, and that I will call him back as soon as there are further developments.

I feel that I'm sympathetic to my clients' need for support and personal contact. Still, I have to juggle an extremely busy schedule, involving many clients. Thus there are times when it may take a day or more to return a phone call.

While an attorney's role does overlap into emotional areas, even the most understanding lawyer cannot and should not replace a therapist. The reality is that the services of a competent mental health professional cost far less than those of a good marital attorney. Many clients would be better served by seeking out this kind of professional help. That said, I believe that every client has a right to expect a reasonable amount of attention from his or her attorney. You should not feel that you're of secondary importance or that your case is being put on the back burner. If you honestly believe that to be the case on a continuing basis, you may want to consider changing attorneys.

Organizing Your Search

Now that you know what to look for in an attorney, let's talk about putting together a list of qualified professionals to interview. Even if you really feel good about the first attorney you meet, you may wish to interview with another attorney before making your final choice.

At this point, I think I can anticipate your next question: "I've never gone through a divorce before, so naturally I'm not in touch with any attorneys who do family law. How, then, do I go about finding the right person to represent me?" There are many qualified professionals out there, and it's not going to be that difficult for you.

The most obvious method that comes to mind is to use personal referrals. Perhaps you have a close friend or relative who has been through a divorce. You may consider asking that person to put you in touch with his or her lawyer—assuming he or she was pleased with how the case was handled. I must caution you, however, that there are some potential problems with this approach.

In the first instance, you may not be ready to tell your friends and family that a divorce is in the wind. News like this has a way of getting around, and you may feel that it's not yet time to publicize it. Furthermore, the circumstances of your case may be substantially different from your friend's. Perhaps her case was relatively straightforward, while yours has all sorts of potential complications. In that event, the attorney who served your friend well may not be able to do the same for you. Finally, there is the delicate issue of jealousy and competition. Maybe your relative or friend came out on the short end of the stick and doesn't want to see you fare any better. I'm not trying to be cynical, but it's important to assess someone's motivations for trying to help you.

On balance, referrals from friends and relatives should certainly be considered. Still, I wouldn't limit myself to those sources. If you do decide to act on this kind of referral, make certain the attorney in question is still actively involved in the marital field.

Another very good source of referrals are other attorneys.

While the lawyer who handled the closing of your house may not be appropriate to handle your divorce, he or she may be able to recommend one or more good people who regularly practice in the family law field. Here again, you may not want to reveal your intentions to your family attorney. But perhaps you are acquainted with a lawyer socially or through business who can help you with some referrals.

If, for one reason or another, you are not able to obtain referrals through professional or personal contacts, don't worry. There are still other options available. Obviously, you can consult the yellow pages and look for attorneys whose ads indicate that they practice in the area of divorce or marital law. Frankly, I find this approach a little too chancy. Attorneys, within certain limits, can write pretty much anything they want in ads. That's why I'd like to see you take a more prudent course of action.

A better option is asking your local bar association for a reference list of attorneys who handle marital cases. They will be glad to help you, although they cannot express a preference for one attorney over another.

There are also various sourcebooks in your local public or university library that list names of attorneys and their areas of practice. There you will find a book called *Martindale-Hubbell Legal Directory*.[1] This is a directory of eight volumes that provides basic information about lawyers and their fields of practice.

While you're at it, you may also want to consult a book called *Who's Who in American Law*.[2] The American Bar Association has also compiled a book containing the names and credentials of over 20,000 litigators in the United States. The book is entitled *Directory of Litigation Attorneys*.[3] In addition, the American Academy of Matrimonial Lawyers publishes a directory[4] that lists by state attorneys who are fellows in that organization and whose primary area of practice is family law.

Aside from looking into reference sources, talking to personal and professional contacts, and consulting your local bar association, you can call or write to organizations such as Parents Without Partners, Legal Awareness for Women, or other local support groups for divorced or divorcing people that meet at religious and community centers.

The Initial Consultation

Once you've organized your list of attorneys, it's time to start calling and setting up interviews. Once you and the attorney settle on a mutually convenient time, you should ask whether or not you'll be charged for the interview. Each attorney has his own policy with respect to this matter—even partners in the same firm. Let me briefly summarize the differing perspectives of two attorneys at the same firm.

Attorney #1: I frequently don't charge for an initial interview—particularly when someone is referred by another attorney or a former client.

Attorney #2: I feel differently than does my colleague, though I certainly respect what he's saying. I do charge for the first consultation, since I am devoting an hour or two to the prospective client.

For me, both viewpoints are valid, though I believe that more attorneys charge for the initial interview than do not. My practice is to charge for the initial conference.

In many ways, it is analogous to the way physicians practice. If you go to a doctor for an examination, that physician is going to examine you and render an opinion. You may be sick or perfectly healthy. You may or may not require surgery. If you do require surgery, you may or may not choose to use that doctor. Whatever happens, you are invariably going to pay a fee for the examination and initial consultation.

Frankly, I don't feel that the issue of charging for the first interview should influence your choice one way or the other. Yes, it may cost you a few hundred dollars before you're able to make an educated choice. But the difference between selecting the right or wrong attorney to represent you can easily save you many thousands of dollars.

Whatever you do, don't let the cost of initial interviews prevent you from considering meeting with two attorneys. If you're going to make an informed choice, it's important that you speak to more than one person. I've met clients for the first time, and we hit it off so well that they didn't want to interview anyone else. Although this is flattering, I sometimes still suggest that they see one other attorney before making a final decision.

Evaluating an Attorney's Personal and Professional Style

Far more important than whether or not an attorney bills you for an initial interview is the way that professional is going to handle your case. Since you are the captain of this particular ship, what kind of a navigator do you want? Would you prefer someone who will stick to safe routes in calm waters? Or would you prefer working with someone who will steer you right into the eye of the storm?

Let's be clear about just how important your choice of an attorney can be to the ultimate outcome of your case. Even though you may be in a position of weakness relative to your spouse, if you have the better lawyer the balance could shift in your favor. After all, it's the lawyers who try the case and do the hard negotiating in contested divorces—not the spouses.

But here again, you and your spouse are in charge—not the attorneys. If two people really want to have an amicable divorce, it's entirely possible. On the other end of the spectrum are those couples who are out for blood. These people tend to seek out the most belligerent kind of lawyer—someone who is going to deal in scorched earth. Couples who are of this frame of mind are not at all interested in lawyers with whom they can feel comfortable. They are looking for a bomber or a barracuda.

Forget about being fair and equitable. Forget about concern for the children. These people are out for revenge. To achieve that, they will retain a lawyer whose only consideration is victory at any cost.

Most people would be wise to avoid the bombers or barracudas of the legal profession. Taking such an aggressive tack will force your spouse to do the same. Then you'll have your all-out war. But when the smoke clears, you're likely to be licking your emotional wounds, trying to repair your children's emotional scars, and counting your financial losses—for many years to come.

I'm happy to say that most competent attorneys are able to adjust to the shifting tides of a case. They can be amicable or tough—as the situation requires. But remember, your attorney, within the bounds of professional ethics and judgment, will be guided to a large extent by your wishes and attitudes. That's why it's important to maintain a rational perspective at all times, as difficult as that might be.

In evaluating attorneys, it's essential to recognize that they also have egos and are subject to a wide range of emotions. From a practical point of view, divorce attorneys are trying to establish their position against other lawyers. This battle for positioning is being fought in a competitive industry by men and women who are competitive by nature.

Most successful litigating attorneys get a certain amount of pleasure from fighting and winning the good fight. I know that I do. This is an important attribute that any good advocate brings to the negotiating table or to the trial of a case. Nevertheless, attorneys have an obligation not to let their own egos overshadow the interests of their clients.

However, I have seen more instances than I care to remember in which an attorney has become so embroiled in a game of one-upmanship that the interests of the client became a secondary consideration. More than anything else, the lawyer just wanted to teach the adversary on the other side that he or she can't be taken advantage of. Unfortunately, the war was being waged at the client's expense.

Now, when you make an up-front decision to work with an attorney, there's no way to be sure what the future will bring. But there are some things you can go on, such as the person's reputation and your own sense of how he or she operates.

If somewhere down the road your evaluation proves to be incorrect, you have every right to switch attorneys in midstream.

As long as your bill is paid in full, the discharged attorney has an obligation to cooperate with you and your new counsel. Again, the bottom line is that within the bounds of professional judgment, ethics, and time availability, your lawyer works for you. If he or she isn't doing the job to your satisfaction, you owe it to yourself to reconsider your choice.

Checklist for Selecting and Working with Attorneys

I'm going to conclude this section with a questionnaire that you can refer to in making your choice of an attorney to handle your divorce. There also are some questions pertaining to your satisfaction. As your case progresses, it may be a good idea to go over your answers to see if they still apply.

Is This the Right Lawyer for Me?

1. How did I contact this person?
2. Is there a charge for the initial interview?
3. What did the attorney do to establish his or her reputation?
4. How much of the attorney's practice is devoted to marital work?
5. Does the attorney seem to understand and empathize with my situation?
6. Does the attorney seem like somebody I will be able to communicate with over a long period of time?
7. Did the attorney answer all my questions directly and honestly?
8. What is the attorney's hourly fee?
9. How much of a retainer will the attorney require?
10. How will subsequent charges be billed?
11. How are telephone conversations billed?
12. How is travel time billed?
13. What is included in my charges for *disbursements*?

14. Am I able to get through to the attorney on the phone?
15. Does it seem as though my case is a priority—or am I being shunted to the back burner?
16. Am I pleased with the way my case is being handled?
17. Will my attorney keep me advised about what is happening on the case? Will I receive copies of correspondence, reports of phone calls, and copies of legal papers as the case progresses?
18. Am I pleased with the results being obtained on my case?
19. Are my expectations about my case or my attorney reasonable?
20. Am I happy with my selection of an attorney?

Notes

1. Available from: Martindale-Hubbell, Inc., 630 Central Avenue, New Providence, NJ 07974, (201) 464-6800. See bibliography.
2. Available from: Marquis Who's Who, Macmillan Directory Division, 3002 Glenview Road, Wilmett, IL 60091. See bibliography.
3. Available from: Prentice-Hall Law and Business, 910 Sylvan Ave., Englewood Cliffs, NJ 07632, (800) 223-0231. See bibliography.
4. Available from: American Academy of Matrimonial Lawyers, 20 North Michigan Avenue, Suite 540, Chicago, IL 60602, (312) 263-6477. See bibliography.

5

Dividing Up
the Marital Pie

Adam and Gloria

One of the first questions new clients invariably ask is: "How am
I going to come out of this financially?" Unfortunately, the answer I have to give most people is this: "Chances are, you won't
be as well off as you would be if you weren't getting a divorce."

You've probably heard the expression, "Two can live as
cheaply as one." That adage applies primarily to couples who are
living together. But when married people decide to split up, all
sorts of costly practicalities come into play. The case of Adam
and Gloria is a good example of what often happens in terms of
family finances. But first, let me give you the overall picture.

Adam is a forty-year-old, self-employed architect who, after
years of struggling, now earns approximately seventy thousand
dollars a year. His thirty-six-year-old wife, Gloria, is a college
graduate who taught elementary school before she and Adam
married some ten years earlier. Eight years ago, they bought a
three-bedroom home in Rockland County—a suburban community about twenty miles north of Manhattan.

After two years of marriage, the couple's first child, David,
was born. At that point, Gloria gave up her teaching job to become a full-time mother and homemaker. Three years later, the
couple had their second child, a daughter named Rachel.

   As the years went by, this once-happy couple started growing
apart. Gloria was often angry because she felt that Adam was too
involved with his work and didn't help enough with raising the
children. And though she was a devoted mother, Gloria was
starting to feel hemmed in—trapped by a life that was becoming
more boring and one-dimensional with each passing day.

   After seven years as a full-time homemaker, Gloria wanted
to devote more time and energy to her own personal develop-
ment. She had always planned to go back to school for her master's degree. Maybe this would be a good time to start pursuing
that goal. In any event, she knew that something in her life had
to change.

   Adam was having his own problems, so he had little attention
to give to his wife's complaints. He had been going through a
difficult transition in his business, which was causing him a lot
of stress. And, unfortunately, there was no end in sight.

   In order to get his new architectural concept off the ground,
Adam had to forgo a number of high-paying assignments.
Money would be tight for another year or two. And even then,
there was no guarantee that he would ever see the kind of economic daylight he sought.

   In the meantime, Adam wanted to dip into the couple's joint
savings account to finance his move to a larger studio. Gloria had
inherited seventy thousand dollars when her mother died—only
a few weeks after the marriage. This made up the bulk of their
savings.

   At first, Gloria kept her inheritance money in her own name,
but shortly after David was born, she transferred the money to
a joint certificate of deposit account. At the time, Gloria didn't
fully understand the impact of what she was doing. It seemed to
her that if two people were really committed to building a life
together, it would be wrong to hold anything back.

   After a while, both Gloria and Adam started thinking of that
money as their family nest egg—something for a rainy day. Now,
that day was here, at least from Adam's point of view. Why
shouldn't he use the money? If his new concept materialized, it
would benefit Gloria and the kids as much as it would him. Still,
Adam sensed that this wasn't the greatest time to broach the issue with his wife.

   Gloria was already disturbed about Adam's lack of attention

to her problems and by his increasing obsession with work. Now he wanted to use her inheritance money to become even more involved in his business—and even less responsive to her needs. In fact, Gloria had been toying with the idea of using some of that money to cover her tuition expenses.

After a few tense discussions, a compromise was reached. Gloria would agree to Adam's using ten thousand dollars of their savings to get his design concept off the ground, if he agreed to go with her to a marriage counselor. Adam accepted this condition, though he didn't see how their problems were any worse than those of their friends.

As far as Adam was concerned, everything hinged on the success of his business. Once things were better financially, the rest would fall into place. At that point, Gloria could go back to school or do anything else she wanted.

"I'm starting to feel as if I have no life of my own," Gloria told the marriage counselor at their first session. "All I do is housework, and that's just not enough to sustain me as a person. I don't necessarily want to go back to school on a full-time basis, although that's certainly a possibility. At the very least, I'd like to take a few courses, pursue my interest in music, and, perhaps, find some new interests."

Adam acknowledged his wife's need for more intellectual stimulation. But he also raised some practical concerns. "I have to work long hours to earn enough to pay the bills," he told the counselor. "Unfortunately, there isn't that much time left to help Gloria with taking care of the house and raising the kids. If she really wants to spend a significant number of hours away from home, she'll probably have to find some kind of job so that we can afford the cost of child care. Otherwise, we'll drain what's left of our savings in no time."

Adam and Gloria dropped out of marriage counseling after two sessions. They had started to air their feelings, but nothing was actually resolved.

Gloria did start taking music lessons and a graduate course at a local college, but, unfortunately, the basic problems continued. Adam began spending more and more time at his new studio. Sometimes he would leave at seven in the morning and return home well after midnight.

Adam always had a legitimate excuse for his long hours. "I'm doing it for you and the kids," he would tell Gloria. Still, as the weeks and months passed, Gloria grew more and more resentful of Adam's time away from the family.

As the relationship between husband and wife deteriorated, Adam found himself spending even more time in and around his new studio. He had become friendly with Norma, a twenty-five-year-old designer whose studio was in the same building.

At first, they just went out for coffee or a casual dinner. There was an undeniable mutual attraction. One night, about two months after they met, Adam and Norma decided to dine at an intimate, candlelit restaurant. They ordered a bottle of wine with dinner, then another. Soon, they were holding hands and snuggling. Two hours later, they were making love in her Manhattan apartment.

As Adam drove back to his picturesque suburban home, his head was spinning. Sex hadn't been this good with Gloria for years. He closed his eyes and tried to go back in his mind. Maybe it had never been this good. "Hey, slow down, guy," he told himself. "You've got a family to think about. Do you really want to break it up because of one good roll in the sack?"

But as it turned out, this was not a one-time fling. Soon, Adam and Norma were having their after-dinner forays three and four times a week. As things started becoming more serious, Adam felt uncertain about handling what was quickly becoming a double life. Nevertheless, he saw no need to make a choice—not yet anyway. "I'll just find a way to keep both relationships together," Adam told himself. "I'll stay with my family, but I'll continue to see Norma as much as possible."

Gloria, for her part, didn't perceive any radical change. Adam was coming home later and later, but she accepted his work-related explanations. Naturally, this meant that there was even less time for them to talk and work at improving their relationship. Still, what was Gloria to do? At least she had started taking some classes and was seeing more friends during the day.

After a while, Gloria decided that things just weren't going to get much better between them until Adam got this new business concept off the ground. But she had taken her marriage vows for better or for worse. Right now, she was experiencing some of the "worse."

Gloria also couldn't help but notice that their sex life had become virtually nonexistent. One night, she dreamed that Adam was having an affair with another woman, but she decided not to ask him about it. They might be having their problems, but Gloria implicitly believed in Adam's honesty and integrity.

As Norma and Adam continued to sleep together, their emotional involvement grew. Before long, Norma was becoming dissatisfied with a lover who always had to return to his wife. At the same time, Adam was starting to view his half-hour drive home as a descent from heaven into hell.

Some nights he'd lie awake, staring at Gloria. If only the lines of communication could have remained open, maybe all of this wouldn't have happened. They had once been so happy. But now, it was as if a wall of ice had come between them. Still, how could he just pick up and leave her and the kids? If only there was a way to make his wife understand that what he really needed was for her to give him the same kind of love and excitement he was now getting from his lover.

As the months passed, the dichotomy in Adam's life continued to grow. On one hand, he had Norma, a sexy and loving companion who understood and supported his dreams. Then there was Gloria, waiting at home with her cold stares and her barely hidden hostility. Adam's choices seemed to be coming into sharper focus.

But what about the kids? Adam dreaded the thought of living away from them. Still, would it really be better for them if their father remained in an unhappy marriage? No matter what happened, he would always love and care for David and Rachel. Still, he had his own life to get on with. He was forty now—not old, but no spring chicken either. He'd better take his shot at happiness while it was still available.

Almost a full year had passed since that first night Adam and Norma made love. Things were pretty much status quo with Gloria, but Norma was pressing him to make a decision. Adam wanted to act, but he felt frozen. The thought of telling Gloria of his affair paralyzed him with guilt and fear. What would he say? That his marriage vows meant nothing? That her years of faith and trust in him amounted to little more than a bad joke?

Inevitably, Adam's thoughts returned to how awful the ordeal of a divorce would be on the children, and the whole package would become even more overwhelming for him to handle. But what was he going to do? He had promised Norma that he would take definitive action, one way or the other. He could no longer put off the inevitable.

Suddenly, a thought occurred to him. Maybe his marriage could be saved after all. He would come clean to Gloria about his affair with Norma. But maybe he could help her understand that their situation forced him to turn elsewhere for something that had disappeared from their marriage. If only she would see the light, things could be good between them once again. He would do whatever it took. They could go back to marriage counseling and really make it work this time.

Now, the human mind can play funny tricks on itself. When we get desperate enough, we can delude ourselves into believing almost anything. And so, Adam had this false sense of elation and euphoria as he sat there pondering his course of action.

It was 10:00 P.M. on a Sunday night. Gloria had just put the kids to sleep. Adam had prepared a pot of tea and was filling both their cups as she walked into the dining room. It seemed like months since he was home early enough for them to enjoy a quiet evening together.

"Sit down and relax," Adam said warmly. "I'd like to talk." Gloria had a good feeling. Adam's business plans had really started jelling lately. Maybe the time had finally come for them to start getting their marriage back on track.

It took less than five minutes for Adam to say the words that shattered Gloria's world. Oh, he dressed them up in a veneer of hope for a reconciliation. But the facts that lay before Gloria were naked and ugly. Her husband had been sleeping with another woman for a whole year. He had lied and deceived her. While she was playing the fool, waiting for things to improve, he was taking his pleasure in someone else's bed. Gloria had heard enough for now. That night, Adam slept on the couch, while Gloria cried herself to sleep in the bed they had shared.

It was only a matter of days before Gloria's depression turned into bitterness. A vindictive anger began to take root. As she saw it, Adam had ruined her life. He had shown himself to be someone with no sense of honor. Even worse, he obviously had no regard for their kids.

As far as Gloria was concerned, the marriage was beyond saving. She wanted this creep out of her life as soon as possible, and divorce was the best way to achieve that goal. Ten days after Adam had invited her to join him in a cup of tea, Gloria retained a well-respected attorney.

Adam was shocked by how quickly his wife was moving. Nevertheless, with Norma's encouragement, he started interviewing attorneys, and wound up retaining a very competent one.

One of the first things Adam asked his lawyer was: "How am I going to come out of this financially?" The answer he received was honest but less than optimistic: "When the smoke clears, you'll probably be far worse off than you would have been if all this had never happened."

I think it would be most instructive if we went through an evaluation of the respective financial positions of both spouses point by point.

Because Adam and Gloria live in New York, the division of their assets is subject to the law of *equitable distribution.* Since over forty states now have such a law on the books, the general concepts I am going to outline will apply to most of you. As we discussed in chapter 2, however, even among the forty or so states, there are differences in approach to dividing property such as interspousal gifts, professional licenses, academic degrees, property acquired before marriage, and the increase in value of *separate property.*

By using the case of Adam and Gloria as a model, you will have an opportunity to explore the mix of factors that come into play. At the same time, I will cover some other common financial problems that divorcing couples often encounter. But first, let's look at the overriding concepts that provide the framework for dividing *marital property* in most states.

Equitable Distribution: What Does It Mean?

The principle of *equitable distribution* provides that all *marital property*—property acquired during the marriage—is subject to division as part of the financial settlement upon divorce. On the other hand, *separate property*—property acquired by a spouse be-fore the marriage—inherited property, or property acquired as a gift from someone other than the spouse are not generally con-sidered part of the settlement, unless there is a specific premar-ital contract in effect that provides for the division of such prop-erty. The increase in value during marriage of one spouse's premarital property may, in some instances, be considered mar-ital and distributed upon divorce.

Most states that now have equitable distribution laws previ-ously divided marital property based on title. That's why they were called *title property states.* Let's explore that concept for a moment, and see how it differs from *equitable distribution.*

When a couple divorced in a *title property state,* the spouse in whose name property existed kept that property after the di-vorce. Therefore, if a business or stock in a business was in your name, you kept it. If the house was in your wife's name, she kept that.

The basic obligations that a husband had in a pre-equitable distribution divorce was to pay *alimony* to the wife for her entire life and to pay child support until the children reached their majority. That was pretty much it.

The change by most states to *equitable distribution* laws repre-sents an acknowledgment that marriage is, indeed, an economic partnership. The legislatures that passed the statutes were send-ing a message to the courts: start looking at the economic part-nership of marriage in the same way as a business partnership.

When a business partnership breaks up, subject to the agree-ment, each of the partners walks away with a certain piece of the pie—assuming that there is a pie to divide. That principle now also applies to the breakup of a marriage.

The whole concept of *equitable distribution* is relatively new, and there still are a great deal of refinements to work out. But, in principle, *equitable distribution* represents a big improvement over dividing property according to who has title. Nevertheless, we still have a long way to go before the law can be deemed anywhere near completely fair and equitable in these matters.

One of the problems involves determining just what consti-tutes an equitable settlement. Is it the same for the working and the nonworking wife? Is it the same for the marriage of three years as for that of thirty years? Is it the same for the forty-five-year-old spouse as for one who is sixty-five? There is no single answer—but, rather, a delicate balancing act is needed.

Let me give you an example of the kinds of things with which the courts must grapple. One inequity that the new laws are trying to set right involves the position of the divorcing wife who has sacrificed her own career and worked, for example, to put her husband through law or medical school. A fairly typical situation of this kind would involve two college sweethearts who marry upon graduation. The wife wants to go to graduate school for her Ph.D. in psychology, while the husband has been accepted to medical school. The couple decides that their mutual goals would be best served if the wife worked until the husband became a practicing doctor. At that point, she would return to school to obtain her degree.

The wife is disappointed to learn that she cannot find a job commensurate with her education in the state where her husband is attending school. Since there is a pressing need for money, she accepts a job as a clerk for the Motor Vehicle Bureau. In addition, she works as a cashier in a supermarket two nights a week in order to bring in a little more money.

Five years go by. The husband graduates from medical school, completes his internship, and is licensed to practice medicine. The wife, who is now twenty-seven, figures that it's now her turn to be a full-time student while her husband works to support her. But there's a hitch. One night, the husband comes home and announces that he wants a divorce. Let's evaluate the wife's likely position under the old and new laws.

In a *title property state*, the wife would, in all likelihood, receive alimony. In the hypothetical case I just outlined, there are no children, so child support would not be a factor. But the key point to consider is that, under the old system, the wife would have no claim whatsoever to be specifically compensated for the time and effort she put into launching her husband's medical career.

In some states, under the concept of *equitable distribution*, however, we're looking at a completely different situation. If this case went to court in New York, the wife would stand a good chance of being considered a partner in her husband's future medical practice. Therefore, she would probably be awarded a percentage of his projected earnings during the life of his practice. Typically, this would amount to several hundred thousand dollars. In most states, however, while the wife may be liable for the debts incurred by the husband in obtaining his degree, she would not benefit from his license or from his increased future earning ability.

Understandably, the wife comes to the conclusion that her husband had been planning his moves for some time. Maybe he did have it in his mind to end the marriage as soon as he received his medical license. Unfortunately, there is no way for the wife to prove this. And even if there was, the chances are better than not that the judge would not take it into consideration in determining the distributive award.

In many states the assertion of wrongdoing on the part of one of the spouses doesn't play a role in the property settlement. Even in fault states, it is doubtful that the husband's questionable course of action would be given much consideration in determining the distributive award.

No, the key issue in the case I just outlined revolves around the parties' relative contributions to the marital pot. Because of the way the current law is being interpreted, the burden of proof rests with the nonmonied spouse, the wife in this case, to establish the value of her contribution to her husband's future.

At the same time, a judge must also deal with a raft of related complications in such cases. One difficulty is determining the value of the degree itself as opposed to the value of the husband's ongoing medical practice. Another is determining when the value of the degree and of the practice merge together. In any event, the wife in this example is likely, in many states, to receive much more than she would under the old title laws, which, at this writing, are only applicable in the state of Mississippi.

As I noted earlier, wives are now receiving on average about 30 to 40 percent of the marital pie. Still, there is a great deal of pressure on the courts to interpret the concept of *equitable distribution* as a presumption of equal distribution—unless there are specific reasons for doing otherwise—and upon the legislatures to enact such a law.

If this were to take effect, we would be looking at something very similar to what is now operative in the nine *community property* states. In general, in those states marital assets are presumed to belong equally to both spouses.

At this writing, assets are divided equitably—not equally—in *equitable distribution* states. In some cases, there may be a 60 to 40 percent division. In other instances, the division may be 80 to 20 percent or even 90 to 10 percent. In any case, there are three main areas to consider in terms of a financial settlement: 1) the distributive award; 2) spousal maintenance; and 3) child support.

I'll discuss spousal maintenance and child support in subsequent chapters. For now, I want to look at how marital assets are divided—in general, and in the case of Gloria and Adam, the couple discussed previously.

Determining What Goes into the Marital Pot

The first thing a divorcing couple needs to ascertain is what are the marital assets. Once this is determined, the parties—or the court—can get down to the business of working out a fair and equitable division.

Let's take a look at what the marital pot contains. Most *equitable distribution* states define marital property as all property acquired during the course of the marriage, regardless of whose name it is in which that property is held. Let's see how this concept applies to some typical assets.

Gifts

When Adam's attorney started inquiring about which property was separate and which was subject to distribution, he asked if Adam had ever given his wife any substantial gifts or presents.

Adam answered that he gave his wife two expensive rings: an engagement ring six months before the nuptials, and a wedding band when the couple took their vows.

While both of those rings are gifts, they are viewed differently from the perspective of *equitable distribution*. The engagement ring was given before the marriage, so it's not marital property. Technically, that piece of jewelry was a gift from someone other than the husband. Therefore, the wife keeps the engagement ring.

The wedding band was given after the justice of the peace asked the couple to say, "I do." The moment a couple takes their vows, and the husband slips the ring on the wife's finger, that piece of jewelry becomes marital property.

In terms of gifts, the dividing line is crystal clear. If Adam had given Gloria the engagement ring even one minute before they were legally married, he still would have no claim to it.

By the same token, the expensive Rolex watch Gloria gave Adam for their fifth anniversary goes into the marital pot because it is a gift from one spouse to the other. The top-end stereo equipment given to Adam as a present by his uncle two years ago, however, is not subject to distribution—as long as it was clearly a gift to him (and not to the couple) by a third party.

INHERITANCE

As with gifts, property acquired by either party through inheritance is not considered part of the distributive award. Therefore, the pearl necklace and rubies Gloria received from her mother as part of her inheritance does not go into the marital pie. Remember, the same principle applies even if she received the jewelry before her mother passed away.

Adam received a five-thousand-dollar bond when his father died. He kept it in his name, and never transferred it to joint names. Therefore, that bond and its proceeds belong solely to him. Why? Because he kept that inherited asset solely in his name throughout the marriage.

You may recall that Gloria inherited seventy thousand dollars upon her mother's death, which she placed into a joint savings account shortly after their first child was born. The moment she transferred those funds into an account bearing her husband's name, she turned (or transmuted) her *separate property* into *marital property*. By doing so, she made her husband a partner in that particular asset.

When Gloria's attorney explained this to her, she was distraught. "What if I took that money out of the joint account," she asked, "and placed it back into a separate account?"

Gloria's counsel had to explain that once *separate property* is transmuted into *marital property,* the process is irreversible with respect to *equitable distribution.*

Remember, it matters not where the inherited money comes from: earnings, stock dividends, or interest income. Once it is placed into any kind of joint account, it becomes the property of both partners, and is, therefore, part of the distributive award.

RETIREMENT PLANS AND PENSIONS

Since Adam was self-employed, he was not eligible for any kind of pension. However, his accountant established a *Keogh plan* when he was twenty-five. Even during the tough times, Adam made it a point to put as much money as he could into his tax-deferred account, which he always kept in his own name.

Adam realized that his wife was going to receive a large percentage of the distributive award, but he had assumed that this retirement nest egg would be his and his alone. When his lawyer told him otherwise, Adam had a stricken look on his face.

"I'm really upset," he told his attorney. "I've worked damn hard for that retirement money and I always kept it in a separate account. Somehow, I was hoping that would be untouchable. I know that the next few years are going to be tough financially, but I was planning to use my retirement money as a cushion for my old age."

Adam's lawyer informed him that this was not the case. One way or another, Gloria would be entitled to a share of that particular asset. "But that's unfair," Adam protested. "I've been busting my tail all these years. Meanwhile, she stayed home and took care of the kids. I realize that's worth something. But don't tell me it's the same kind of labor I put into running my business." In the meantime, Gloria's attorney was quite correct in assuring her that she would be a full participant when it comes time to divide up the marital assets—including her husband's retirement plan.

The courts are making it increasingly clear that a wife's labor in taking care of a home and bringing up children is worth the same amount economically as the husband's labor in going out to work. This is a reality that men like Adam must learn to face. All monies earned by him are distributable, and a retirement plan or pension are simply deferred earnings. Therefore, the money in such plans is included in the marital pot.

Let's look at a few other points on the issue of pensions, which differ slightly from retirement accounts. For example, a teacher's pension for someone earning thirty-five thousand dollars a year and retiring after twenty years is often based on receiving half of their last year's salary. In fact, the actual value of that pension is much more. A pension of this kind can be worth hundreds of thousands of dollars, depending on a person's age and how long he or she is going to be around to collect.

In terms of assessing the value of a pension, a computation could be made based on life expectancy and on the cumulative dollars one would be likely to receive down the road. The spouse could receive a percentage starting at the time the pension is distributed, or the spouse could choose to buy out the interest in a pension based on its present value.

Although I don't think it's necessary to burden you with further particulars, you can assume that your spouse is your partner in virtually every aspect of your financial life. As we've seen, that includes your business or professional practice, your bank accounts, pension, tax shelters, stock holdings, real estate investments, and personal property. On the other side of the coin, the marital debts that are outstanding are also the responsibility of both parties, even though the credit card or loan may be in only one spouse's name. But there's still one kind of asset we haven't discussed.

THE FAMILY HOME

For many American families, the home in which they live represents their greatest asset—as well as a roof over their heads. Small wonder that this single piece of marital property is often the core issue in negotiating the division of the marital pie.

Viewed simply as a tangible asset, the marital home is very much like other kinds of property. In many instances, the simplest solution is to sell the home and divide the proceeds. Indeed, the cost of divorce can be so expensive that some families have no other choice.

But what if there are school-age children? In that instance, selling the home would only exacerbate an already highly disruptive situation. What if there are younger children and the newly divorced mother is reentering the job market for the first time in years? Here again, a mandated sale of the family home would only salt the wounds.

In these cases, many courts make a distinction between occupancy and ownership. Therefore, even though the husband may have been awarded a one-half (or even greater) interest in the marital home, a judge may grant the wife occupancy for an extended period of time—particularly if she has been awarded custody of the children.

Unfortunately, such judicial rulings can only benefit those families who don't immediately need the proceeds from the sale of the house. In many instances, the marital home must be sacrificed so that there is enough money left to set up two separate households.

Gloria and Adam found themselves in just such a quandary. Adam wanted to get a big enough place to accommodate his girlfriend, with room for the children, who would stay with him on alternate weekends. This would make it impossible for him also to support the mortgage payments and taxes on the house.

Thus, the house must be put up for sale; however, the market is soft, and the estranged couple will probably be forced to settle for a price that is, perhaps, a third lower than they could get under favorable circumstances.

When the smoke clears, this once-functional family unit will be living in two relatively cramped apartments, paying two rents that amount to significantly more than the monthly payment on their comfortable home, and thousands of dollars will have been spent on legal fees and relocation expenses.

Adam is going to be disappointed to find that, even though his business is now thriving, he has far less disposable income.

Between *maintenance* and *child support* payments, his new lifestyle will be far less carefree than his old one. Furthermore, it is likely that his wife will receive a substantial share of the value of his business, and even though he will be paying out Gloria's distributive share over a period of time, his cash flow still will be reduced.

On the surface, Gloria's immediate financial prospects don't seem quite as glum. She'll be able to go back to school. Nevertheless, she's not likely to be gloating over her circumstances. The new apartment she'll be moving into won't be nearly as spacious nor as comfortable as the house she'll soon be leaving. Obviously, the children are going to be affected as well by the depleted financial resources.

Adam and Gloria were planning to send the kids to private schools. That idea will have to be scrapped now, as will sleepaway summer camp. David needs braces for his teeth. That's just going to have to wait, as will the piano lessons Rachel was supposed to start in the fall.

Okay, you're probably wondering what the bottom line is to all this. I'm certainly not suggesting that you don't divorce if you think it's appropriate. But I want you to understand and appreciate the kind of financial turmoil you're likely to be facing so that you can go into it with your eyes open.

In the case of a two-income couple with no children, it may be possible to come out of an amicable divorce without suffering much financial hardship. But if your situation is anything like Adam and Gloria's, things are bound to get pretty tough before they get better.

Years from now, your finances will restabilize, and you'll be able to look back at divorce as the turning point in your life. But, at least in the short run, you should be prepared to face substantial financial turbulence.

Your Attorney's Role in Obtaining the Best Financial Settlement

As I said at the beginning of this chapter, one of the first things clients ask is: "How much am I going to get? What am I entitled to?" Since they are paying good money for this kind of expertise, people have a right to expect their lawyers to provide these answers. Yet unless the necessary information is at hand, even the best attorney can't offer very meaningful advice.

In order to give you a good idea of where you stand, an attorney first has to ascertain the individual and cumulative value of all marital assets. The process of seeking out that information is called *discovery*.

I find that most people go into a divorce unaware of their rights and entitlements relative to those of their spouse. Therein lies one of the most important purposes of *discovery*—to elucidate, to enumerate, to evaluate, and to expose what is the scope of the marital assets. Once that is determined, an attorney can properly advise his client and help that person make a decision about how to proceed.

Now, there are certain assets that are relatively easy to evaluate. Appraising automobiles, jewelry, and even houses, is fairly routine and inexpensive. However, as we saw earlier, the current value of certain assets—such as a business or a professional practice—can be far trickier.

Attorneys have to walk a fine line between being cost-effective and helping their clients get everything that they have coming. In some instances, attorneys will suggest that clients take certain risks or incur certain expenses in the process of trying to obtain a favorable settlement.

At the same time, it is an attorney's duty to help clients understand that, in most cases, it is simply not cost-effective to attempt to track down every single dollar's worth of marital assets. Doing so can cost you thousands of dollars in appraisal and legal fees. In particularly contentious divorces, I've seen people spend more money hiring appraisers than the actual dollar-value of the assets they were fighting over. The problem, however, often is that a business or professional practice may initially appear to be worth much more than it actually is. Oftentimes, counsel cannot tell the "bottom line" until the fees and costs of the legal investigation and appraisal have already been expended.

It behooves you to encourage counsel to use common sense and sound professional judgment, while keeping you advised as to your rights and entitlements. Please consider the following analogy: A man who is facing criminal charges can make a value judgment that he doesn't want to be represented by counsel. Nevertheless, in order to make that judgment, he also must be fully apprised of his right to be represented by counsel.

In the same way, a client can decide that she's not looking for any part of her husband's pension. Before she can forgo that right, however, she must be aware that she is entitled to part of the pension and what that asset is worth. To make such a decision without the relevant information would not constitute an informed consent. Therefore, it would be unfair to the client.

On the other hand, if the client finds out that the pension in question has a current value of fifty thousand dollars, she can choose to forgo her interest in it. Please don't misunderstand. I'm not suggesting that you give up anything to which you and your attorney feel you're entitled. At the same time, I don't think it's necessary or desirable for divorcing spouses to squeeze each other for every last dollar.

As in any negotiation, there are going to be trade-offs. The wife can make an informed judgment at that point and say, "I don't really need to receive a piece of his pension. As far as I'm concerned, he can keep the whole thing." Or, the husband can decide: "Let her keep her inheritance, even if it was placed in a joint account at one point."

Of course, there are some clients who try to turn the division of assets (and, indeed, the entire divorce process) into an instrument for revenge. They walk in asking me, "How can I nail that jerk?" "How can I make that woman pay?" Clients with an axe to grind are often obsessed with issues of fault. "She cheated on me," they complain. "He was unresponsive in bed." One of an attorney's most difficult tasks is convincing these clients that in most states marital fault plays little part in determining the distribution of marital assets.

Despite all of the intense emotions that go into a divorce, I find that most people really want to be fair. It's not always easy, but the majority of clients eventually come to the conclusion that it's best to be equitable. They may not want to give more than they should, but they're not necessarily out to get more than they deserve.

A good attorney tries to reinforce that instinct for fairness in a client without sacrificing the toughness that's needed to win at this game. The question is: "When is it better to be tough, and when is it better to give a little?" Here again, there are no easy answers.

The entire divorce process can be a stressful ordeal, partly because there are so many decisions to be made and so much uncertainty about the future. Anxiety over finances is, understandably, part of the package.

When you and your spouse were together, your financial situation was comparatively predictable. Now, you're both likely to feel that you're operating in a void. Most people are resilient enough to deal with adversity. Still, facing the unknown is never easy.

Let's assume a wife in a divorce action knows that she's going to get one hundred dollars a week *maintenance* and a lump sum of ten thousand dollars from her husband. She may be unhappy with the settlement and anxious about the future, but at least she has some objective parameters to work with in attempting to restructure her life.

If that same woman were sitting in limbo, uncertain of the outcome, her anxiety level would be much higher. At that point, she might start calling her lawyer every week, demanding, "When are we going to get an offer? When are we going to resolve the case?"

Meanwhile, the attorney fully realizes that he can only weaken his client's position by appearing to be overanxious. But again, counsel can only advise and navigate the ship. If a client insists on settling the case immediately, a lawyer may be hard pressed to do otherwise.

If you want to help your attorney help you get your share of the marital pie, I'd like you to consider three brief closing pieces of advice:

1. The more fully you understand your rights and obligations, the better you're likely to fare.

2. Find an attorney who inspires your confidence, and heed his or her advice.

3. Have patience. Remember, if you're the one pushing too hard for a quick settlement, financial matters are less likely to be resolved in your favor.

6

Spousal and Child Support

I N discussing the dissolution of the financial partnership that transpires in a divorce, we are dealing with three primary elements: 1) the distributive award (covered in chapter 5); 2) *alimony* or *maintenance;* and 3) *child support.*

If you are talking about two working spouses who have no children, *child support,* obviously, does not come into play. As far as *alimony* is concerned, it would tend to be minimal in such situations—if it was to be awarded at all. However, in marriages in which the needs of dependent children are a consideration, you are dealing with a financial package that involves all three factors, and each must be taken into account.

The monied spouse (traditionally the husband) wants to know how much he will have to pay in terms of total dollars. The nonmonied spouse (frequently a wife who will retain custody of the children) is concerned about having sufficient funds to support herself and her dependents in an acceptable fashion. Whatever your position, it is critical to work closely with your attorney in balancing all the relevant factors and in assessing your best settlement options. Let's look at some of the key issues that factor into the equation.

Alimony

Traditionally, a divorcing husband was almost always required to pay some kind of support to his ex-wife for life—or until she remarried. Even if the wife was working full-time, the husband was still obliged to pay something. The only exception to this general rule occurred if the divorce was the result of fault on the part of the wife.

The old alimony concept derived, in part, from gender stereotypes that may seem repugnant today. Nevertheless, the thinking was that the husband functioned as the breadwinner, while the wife's role was to care for the home and raise the children. Upon marriage, the all-powerful husband assumed an obligation to care for his more-or-less helpless wife until she either remarried or died. The old law also assumed that, in general, the wife owned no property and was, therefore, largely dependent on her husband's resources.

There is no question that the antiquated notions that formed the basis of the old alimony laws have lagged behind the societal and interpersonal changes of recent decades. On the other hand, there are those who feel that, in attempting to reflect a more contemporary view by acknowledging women to be on a par with men, the new laws have wound up inadvertently hurting the very wives they were attempting to protect. More about that shortly. But first, let's look at the changes that have taken place with respect to this whole spousal-support concept.

Rehabilitative Maintenance

The statutes, as they exist today, have rendered spousal support to be gender-neutral. This means that, instead of the husband paying the wife, the economically advantaged spouse is required to pay the economically disadvantaged spouse—without regard to the gender of the payor or payee. In addition, in the vast majority of states, marital fault is no longer a bar to the spouse receiving maintenance—nor is it even considered.

As a matter of fact, this gender-neutral concept predates the *equitable distribution* laws in a great many states. Included in these new economic concepts was the idea that spousal support should not necessarily last for a lifetime, rather, it should last for a variable period of time to be determined by a variety of factors. Thus a new concept found its place in the lexicon of a divorce.

The rationale for permanent support was based on the concept that, upon marriage, a husband assumed a lifelong obligation to provide for his wife. In deeming women to be full economic partners, however, the legislatures now presume that both spouses are in an equally good position to take care of themselves.

Part of the intent of rehabilitative maintenance is to acknowledge the independence and financial capability of women. Since they are, at least in theory, full economic partners under the law, why should ex-wives routinely be allowed to receive alimony for the rest of their lives? After all, part of the reason for *equitable distribution* is to empower the less economically advantaged spouse and to make her more independent. It follows, then, that if a couple breaks up, the wife should be expected to become self-supporting within a reasonable period of time.

The main function of *rehabilitative maintenance* is to allow the nonworking spouse an appropriate amount of time to get back on her feet—to provide a bridge period for her to rejoin or enter the work force. The questions are, though, how long should such rehabilitation last, and at what level?

Guidelines for Awarding Maintenance

Under the law of *equitable distribution, maintenance* may be for a short time or for a longer period of time. In some cases, maintenance may last for an entire lifetime. Unlike the old alimony laws, however, no one-size-fits-all time interval is specified. Rather, each case must be evaluated on its own merits and specific circumstances. The following is a list of some of the many factors the courts now use to determine the duration and amount of maintenance:

- The income and property of each spouse—including marital property that is part of the distributive award
- The length of the marriage
- The age and health of the spouses

- The present and future earning capacity of the spouse currently in need of support
- The presence of children in the respective homes of the parties
- The standard of living established during the marriage
- The tax consequences to each of the spouses

Let's look at a few examples that illustrate the application of the above criteria as they apply to the concept of *rehabilitative maintenance*.

• Sixty-year-old Ben has filed to divorce his fifty-eight-year-old wife, Carol. The couple's three children are grown. Two of them now have children of their own. Ben is a successful real estate broker. Carol had worked as a secretary before her marriage, but she has been completely out of the job market for twenty-eight years and has, for all intents and purposes, lost her skills.

Under such circumstances, the court may very well order lifetime maintenance. Consider the thinking behind that determination.

Given Carol's age, as well as her educational and vocational background, she would be likely to find it extremely difficult to reenter the labor force. Although she might be able to find some kind of low-paying work, this would not begin to support the comfortable life-style to which she has grown accustomed.

Based on the way most courts interpret the laws, a husband in Ben's position would have to pay sufficient maintenance to make up that difference. If Carol's career prospects were limited to finding a job at the minimum wage, most judges would be inclined to consider that inappropriate and order Ben to pay full lifetime maintenance. In essence, the outcome of this case is not very different from what it would have been under the old alimony concept.

If, on the other hand, Carol had previously worked as, say, a psychiatrist or an attorney, the court would probably feel that she would have a much greater possibility of becoming self-supportive. Therefore, the maintenance posture may be something less than a totally permanent one.

• Mark and Lynn have been married for two years. Although she has not worked during the marriage, twenty-eight-year-old Lynn had held down responsible positions in the field of personnel ever since graduating from college. Based on her age, her level of skills, and her freedom from the responsibilities of child rearing, one would expect Lynn to be able to resume her previous career in a relatively short period of time.

If this case went to trial, a judge might not order any *maintenance*. Perhaps the court would find it appropriate to award one year's maintenance for bridge purposes. Let's now consider a somewhat more complex case.

• Gary is a forty-six-year-old electrical contractor. His forty-year-old wife, Pat, had worked as an account executive in the advertising field until the birth of their first son, Jeff, some sixteen years earlier. One year later, a second son, Michael, was born. Pat has been a full-time housewife and mother for that entire period.

Pat feels that it is important that she stay home—at least until the two boys graduate high school. At that point, it is expected that Jeff and Michael will either be in college or working full-time, and Pat will feel better able to resume her own career.

Gary sees no reason why Pat can't start working immediately—at least on a part-time basis. His attorney feels comfortable that the court is likely to share that view. I believe he is correct in his assessment of how the issue of maintenance would be resolved if this case went to court.

Under these circumstances, most judges would assume that there was no reason why the wife couldn't eventually resume her career. After all, she is a college graduate with marketable skills. Naturally, she could not be expected to be hired at the level she had previously attained. Still, even as a new trainee, Pat should be able to earn over $20,000 a year.

While Pat is still the boys' primary caretaker, it is no longer necessary for her to always be there when they arrive home from school. In fact, most of today's fifteen- and sixteen-year-olds tend to be extremely independent. In evaluating Pat's job prospects, the court would be looking at a person who has all the necessary attributes to be self-supporting. She is, after all, well-educated, in good health, and her children have no special problems or needs that would require full-time attention for an indefinite period of time.

Most judges would be hard-pressed to conjure up a good reason why Pat can't be out working full-time once the boys are grown and out of the house. Until that happens, she would probably be expected to start working part-time. All things considered, a judge might award *maintenance* for perhaps three or four years. After that, Pat would be expected to make her own way in the world without depending on Gary's resources.

• Let's now consider the case of thirty-seven-year-old Fred and his thirty-four-year-old wife Allison. At the time the divorce action commences, the couple's two daughters, Rebecca and Elizabeth, are nine and seven, respectively. Fred is a life insurance agent. Allison is a college graduate with a degree in social work. Up until the birth of her first child, Allison was a caseworker for a state agency. Since that time, she has not had gainful employment.

Allison has learned that her previous job would no longer be available to her. In fact, she would probably have to complete a master's degree before she could find similar employment. In many cases, the court would make some provision to include educational costs in determining the duration and amount of *maintenance*.

Even if she could manage to attend graduate school, Allison would prefer waiting until both children are out of high school before she seeks full-time employment. And while a judge would certainly be inclined to grant a longer period of rehabilitation in consideration of the children's young ages, it is unlikely that the period and the amount of maintenance would be sufficient to allow Allison to stay out of the job market until the girls are independent.

If she cannot attend school or find a job based on her existing qualifications, Allison may be headed for some hard economic times, given a limited maintenance award. Herein lies the oft-heard criticism that rehabilitative *maintenance*—and, indeed, the whole concept of equitable distribution—is unfair to women.

The thinking behind rehabilitative maintenance is that women are receiving their fair share of an equitable distribution settlement. But, in fact, wives infrequently receive 50 percent of the marital assets upon divorce. And, while in theory the earning power of women is supposed to be equal to that of men, this is yet another fiction.

When you combine the economic impact of an unequal distributive award with the costs involved in maintaining custody of the children, you can see why the situation is particularly tough on nonworking mothers who have devoted most of their productive time to homemaking and child rearing. This is true even when child support is being paid. The wife in the case at hand has a college degree. While she may be forced to obtain more schooling or seek employment in another field, Allison is in a far better position than women of her age with little or no training or job experience. Even so, she is likely to feel economically deprived and battered by the system.

Perhaps some day we will see a true equality between the sexes—not only in our courts, but throughout society. Unfortunately, this is not the case right now. Furthermore, many wives find themselves in a catch-22 situation. Those who do go out and join the work force are often able to find only low-paying jobs. In that case, whatever meager income is brought in results in a lower award of *maintenance*. On the other hand, if a woman does not actively pursue some kind of work, her ex-husband may also be able to use that as grounds for a lower maintenance award.

There is no question that the new divorce laws have produced some inequities that did not exist under the older, and supposedly more sexist, statutes. Indeed, there seems to be a longing in certain circles for those days gone by. Of course, it is impossible to move back in time, nor do I think it is desirable. We find ourselves at a tricky impasse in terms of gender relations, and the courts are reflecting this transition. In any case, there does not seem to be any possibility of turning back the clock.

It is true that the great majority of judges are men. And while most of them do their best to interpret the laws in a fair and just manner, they are as subject to human emotions as the rest of us. A female attorney with whom I was recently discussing this issue made the following pointed observations:

"Many of these male judges—particularly the older ones— are offended by the whole notion of women's liberation. Therefore, they are prone, when awarding *maintenance,* to take the following attitude: 'If you want equal rights, that's fine. But you had better damned well be ready to assume the responsibilities and hardships that go along with those benefits.'

"Since the new laws were supposedly designed to help women, this kind of posture on behalf of the court is ironic— and even tragic in the worst cases."

While I must acknowledge that there is more than a grain of truth in such thoughts, I come back to a precept I repeat throughout these chapters: If you want to achieve a divorce settlement that is truly equitable, do everything in your power to work things out between you and your spouse. Try your best to stay out of court. Don't make the mistake of allowing a judge— or anyone else—to determine your destiny for you.

• George is a thirty-seven-year-old systems analyst who owns stock in his company. He and his thirty-five-year-old wife, Rosemary, mutually agree to divorce. The couple has eight-year-old twin girls. Rosemary left her job in the production department of a large magazine publishing house three months before the twins were born.

As part of the *distributive award,* Rosemary receives one hundred thousand dollars as a cash buy-out of her husband's stock. Because of the age of the children and the need for Rosemary to pursue additional training before she can reenter the job market at her previous level, a maintenance settlement is negotiated in the amount of thirty thousand dollars each year for five years.

You will recall that the amount of distributive award the spouse receives is one of the factors taken into consideration in determining the level of maintenance. Therefore, the hundred thousand dollars offers Rosemary an investment capability that must be factored into the equation.

Let's assume Rosemary takes that money and invests it into a triple-tax-free bond that pays 7 percent. That would provide her with additional income in the amount of seven thousand dollars, which would be roughly equivalent to a taxable income of about ten thousand dollars, based on a tax rate of about one-third. In evaluating the amount of *maintenance* Rosemary receives, a court would almost certainly consider this interest income. Therefore, the parties and their attorneys will also factor this into any settlement they might negotiate.

It is important to think of the financial settlement as three separate but closely interrelated aspects of the whole economic package. A good attorney will take heed of all the relevant factors in attempting to negotiate a favorable settlement on your behalf.

Whatever the specifics, both you and your spouse will be best served in the long run if the ultimate solution is fair and equitable to both of you. Such a settlement will be particularly beneficial to those who stand to be hurt the most by the economic chaos that can occur in the wake of divorce.

Child Support

While the issue of providing economic support for the children of divorcing couples is the third major component of the financial settlement, it is one that deserves primary consideration on the part of estranged parents and their attorneys. Although the issue of *child custody* is distinct from the financial aspects of the case, divorcing couples often find it difficult to separate the following questions:

- Who will care for the children?
- Who will pay for that care?

If there is no other reason to hammer out an economic package that is fair to both parties, the ultimate welfare of the children should provide more than sufficient motivation for all concerned. While spouses with no children can, if they wish, disappear from one another's lives, estranged parents do not have that option—either from a legal or ethical standpoint. Unfortunately, it is impossible to legislate ethics and morality.

It has been variously estimated that about half of all divorced fathers do not pay the full amount of support mandated by their *divorce decree.* Furthermore, the level of court-ordered support has been totally inadequate for many custodial mothers to maintain an acceptable life-style. It was determined in the early 1980s that the average amount of support ordered nationwide did not cover even one-third of what it cost to clothe, feed, and maintain a child. In effect, the courts and deadbeat fathers were conspiring to create a burgeoning population of single-parent families, headed by women who were forced to live on the edge of poverty—if not at the poverty level.

So horrendous was this situation that, in 1984, Congress passed legislation requiring every state to create guidelines for awarding adequate *child support* payments. Though the specifics vary from state to state in terms of the formula used to determine the amount of support, the underlying precepts are basically the same:

• Both parents share the responsibility to contribute to the economic well-being of their children, no matter how low their income. This responsibility does not end when a parent is absent from the household.

• Children should not be made to shoulder unfairly the economic burden brought about by the estrangement of their parents. As much as possible, children should be protected from the overall decline in living standards that results from parents maintaining two households.

What Does It Cost to Support Your Children?

Support guidelines now exist in virtually every state, but judges are not necessarily mandated to follow them. In any event, it is essential for the nonmonied spouse to be aware of the actual costs of supporting children. Additionally, under certain circumstances the spouses can choose to "opt out" or agree to a child support level other than as set forth in the statute. I would strongly suggest that those of you who are anticipating a breakup start keeping a running record of all child-related expenses to establish your real needs. These would include the following:

- Housing
- Food
- Clothing
- Transportation
- Medical and dental care
- School supplies
- Day-care and baby-sitting
- Allowances
- Music or dance lessons
- Summer camp
- Athletic equipment
- Computer and electronic equipment
- Entertainment, games, and gifts
- Extraordinary expenses brought about by special physical or psychological needs

This list is meant as a general guideline for typical child-care expenses. I would strongly suggest that you sit down with your attorney and/or accountant and carefully assess your calculations. You should also be aware that as your children grow older, it generally costs more to support them. Add to this the inevitable effect of inflation, and you can see why a child-support payment that might suffice today may be totally inadequate a few years down the road.

Many custodial mothers who find themselves in this situation try to go back to court in order to obtain increased child support. Unfortunately, this tends to be a tedious and expensive procedure, and the results are unpredictable. An alternative, if child support is not based upon a statutory formula, would be to include anticipated increases in your original settlement. Let your attorney know that you are aware of these factors, and ask him or her to help you deal with them in the most appropriate and effective manner.

As time goes by, there may well be some large unanticipated expenses. One issue that frequently comes up is the escalating costs of a college education. If one of your children is seventeen and college-bound at the time of the divorce, you and your spouse will have to deal with that issue expeditiously.

It is reasonable to assume that, under these circumstances, the monied spouse would foot most of the bill for college, assuming higher education was deemed appropriate by either the court or the parents. Keep in mind, however, that many courts do not consider a college education a child's birthright.

Even if a college education is not mandated, however, it may be something you and your ex-spouse consider desirable. If your children are still in their preteen years, you may want to leave this issue open for later discussion. Another possible solution is for the monied spouse to agree to pay for the children's college education—subject to economic ability to do so down the road.

When it comes to matters concerning your children, it is particularly important that you learn to cooperate with your spouse. Constant parental arguments about support threaten a child's economic and emotional well-being. By thinking of your child's welfare first, you enhance your own chances of emerging a winner. This is not to say that you should make inappropriate financial concessions.

If you and your spouse—through your lawyers or even directly—can come to a mutually acceptable settlement, you can put this thing behind you and go on with your lives. Remember, if you can both assume a rational posture, you don't have to get into a long, dragged-out battle. By resolving things within a reasonable time frame, you won't have to put yourselves or your children through the nightmare of a trial. Still, no matter how amicably you and your spouse behave, there are likely to be some rugged financial waters ahead.

We have looked at some of the hardships that many working as well as nonworking custodial mothers suffer in the wake of divorce. Indeed, women in this position face a severe drop-off in their life-style. Some studies have indicated that such women suffer as much as a 70 percent decline in their living standard, while their husbands enjoy a 40 percent increase in their standard of living.

I must agree that divorcing noncustodial husbands may not suffer as many hardships as their estranged wives. Nevertheless, most family men who fulfill their support responsibilities do not have a particularly easy row to hoe—unless they happen to be financially well-heeled.

Let's take the case of Lou, a forty-year-old technical analyst and his forty-one-year-old wife, Marilyn, who has not worked since the birth of their first son ten years earlier. The couple also has a seven-year-old daughter.

Lou currently earns sixty-five thousand dollars a year—plus extensive health and retirement benefits. Marilyn is a former elementary-school teacher who plans to return to work when the children are older. Lou was the moving party in the divorce. He was having an affair with a thirty-one-year-old woman, with whom he now plans to live.

Now, Marilyn is understandably concerned about the future. Even though Lou is not particularly resistant to the idea of providing adequate *maintenance* and *child support,* there simply is not a great deal of money to go around. The family is living in a three-bedroom house in a suburb known for the quality of its school system, and Marilyn would very much like to remain there, at least for the time being.

Lou would like to accommodate Marilyn's wishes for the children's sake, but it looks like a tall order. The mortgage and taxes on the house are over twelve hundred dollars a month. Even before the divorce action proceeded, there wasn't much slack after all the bills were paid. But now Lou is going to have to bear the cost of another place to live in addition to everything else. He decides to set up an appointment with his attorney in order to discuss his financial prospects. Let's listen in on the attorney's assessment:

"Since your wife isn't working right now, the entire financial burden is going to fall on you, at least for the time being. Sixty-five thousand dollars is a good salary, even if it doesn't go as far as it once did. Still, it provided you with enough to support a comfortable life-style. I'm sorry to tell you that the situation is about to change.

"I don't want to alarm you, Lou, but you had better prepare yourself for some tough economic times. Let me explain that to you. Understand that two people who live apart cannot live nearly as cheaply as they can when they are living together.

"Think about it. You are going to have two rents, two separate basic telephones and two shopping bills. Your wife was able to drive you to the train station and use your car while you were at work. Now you are both going to need cars of your own.

"You mentioned that you and the new woman in your life wanted to take a trip abroad. Frankly, I don't see how you're going to swing it. What I'm basically telling you, Lou, is that it's time for some serious belt-tightening. By the time you get through paying your and your wife's legal expenses—and start maintaining two separate households, you may wind up looking for a second job in order to make ends meet.

"I realize that you want to get a divorce and to start leading your new life. That's your privilege. After all, you are not required to be married to the same person for the rest of your life. Nevertheless, I want you to recognize the financial implications of what you are doing.

"You have indicated that you have no intention of abandoning your two children. I'm very happy to hear that. But again, I want you to fully understand what that's going to mean from an economic standpoint.

"Remember, *child support* in this state continues until the kids turn twenty-one—not eighteen. Your son and daughter are used to a comfortable life-style. You own a large house in a nice suburban area. The schools are very good and the kids both have a lot of friends. I don't know what your thinking is in terms of living arrangements, but it's going to be difficult to ask your wife and kids to move into a small apartment for three hundred dollars a month. Even if you decided to take that course, I doubt very much that the court would allow it.

"You could, of course, sell the house and move your family into a three-bedroom apartment in a comparable area to the one in which they currently reside. But in today's market, that is likely to cost more than the $1,200 you're currently paying in mortgage and real estate taxes. Perhaps it would be better if your wife and children continued living in the house for another six years. It may just be cheaper—and it certainly would be a more stable and comfortable environment for the kids.

"These are value judgments you are just going to have to make. Whatever you decide, however, I want to apprise you of some of the specific consequences of what you are doing:

• The $70,000 in savings that you were counting on as a nest egg for you to get started in your new life probably will not be there.

• The money that your wife would have received by way of interest from her share of the sale of the house is also not going to be there if you decide not to sell. This, in all likelihood, will mean that you will have to pay her more maintenance.

"As we move ahead, we will discuss these issues in greater detail and try to come up with the most productive options. For now, I can only suggest that you would be wise to think in terms of pulling your belt a few notches tighter."

Collecting Unpaid Support

I mentioned earlier that half of all fathers who owe *child support* pay either nothing or less than the full amount originally promised. Some of these men are in a similar position to the husband in our last example. They start out intending to fulfill their obligations, but once the reality of supporting two households sinks in, they decide that they simply cannot cope.

While it is certainly inexcusable to deny one's children the financial support to which they are entitled, I don't think most of these men are inherently bad people. As I've noted before, divorce is a process of mind-boggling complexity. There is a saying: "Out of sight, out of mind." Some men who are less than completely responsible simply tune out their support obligations, hoping they can start anew. Unfortunately, it's not that simple.

Anyone with even a little bit of a conscience cannot simply desert his children without experiencing severe guilt and loss of self-esteem. My advice to men who are tempted to take this course is to reconsider. If the financial terms of your divorce are such that you cannot live with them, ask your spouse to renegotiate the terms, or go back to court and seek a modification. But whatever you do, don't desert your children.

As already stated, a woman trying to collect child support from a recalcitrant ex-husband does not have an easy road. Going to court is an expensive and often futile proposition. Nevertheless, the outlook is not as glum as it once was. If you are having trouble collecting *child support* payments, you can contact your local family court or a branch of your state's Office of Child Support Enforcement (OCSE). This agency has the legal power to attach your husband's salary and other assets in order to satisfy his financial obligation to you. The OCSE can also help you collect unpaid *maintenance,* but only if it is combined with *child support.*

These organizations can prove very helpful—particularly to women whose husbands have salaried jobs. In many cases, the overdue payments are deducted directly from the husband's weekly paycheck. On the other hand, a wife has a much more difficult problem collecting from a self-employed husband. In cases like this, it may be necessary to retain the services of a skilled attorney. If the lawyer you used for your divorce does not have extensive experience in enforcement actions, I would advise you to find one who does. He or she is more likely to be able to work with you in finding hidden assets that can be seized to satisfy child-support obligations.

In many businesses—particularly those with a large volume of cash transactions—there are often facts and manipulations that the principals would rather not have brought to light. Wives often know information about their ex-husbands that can prove useful in motivating them to keep up with their support obligations. An experienced attorney will be able to ask you questions that may elicit important facts.

At that point, you may be able to convince your husband that it is in his best interest to pay the support you and your children are due. I realize that such tactics sound heavy-handed—and, on some level, they are. Nevertheless, if your spouse is sufficiently irresponsible to avoid the financial and moral obligations he has to his children, guerrilla tactics may be warranted—just so long as they stay within the letter of the law.

Balancing the Support Package

The best way to view the financial settlement of your divorce is as a package that includes all aspects of the dollars that you are going to be paying or receiving. If you are the payor, you will want to evaluate exactly how much money you will be paying out in terms of distributive award, maintenance, and support. As the payee, your primary concern will be the total amount available for you and your children to live on.

In a sense, a dollar is a dollar—whether it is paid or received through maintenance or child support. Nevertheless, there are a number of factors to consider from a negotiating standpoint. For one thing, maintenance lasts for a specified period of time and terminates if the spouse remarries. Child support, on the other hand, lasts until the child reaches either eighteen or twenty-one. Furthermore, the payor's financial responsibility to his children continues even if his wife remarries.

"There are also differences in the tax ramifications in maintenance and child support," observes Julian Block, an attorney in Larchmont, New York, and a nationally syndicated columnist and author of *Julian Block's Year-Round Tax Strategies.*[1]

"Maintenance is considered a tax deduction for the payor and taxable income for the payee. Child support, on the other hand, has no tax consequences for either party. Therefore, the paying spouse cannot deduct such payments from his or her income tax. At the same time, the recipient spouse does not have to show those payments as taxable income."

In considering the three aspects of the financial settlement, it is important to sit down with your attorney and evaluate the particulars of your situation. For example, if you are a wife whose husband has proved unreliable in meeting his financial obligations, it may be in your best interests to go for a larger share of the distributive award, while accepting less in alimony and child support.

Essentially, this approach amounts to receiving support and maintenance in advance. Under these circumstances, the husband's attorney may be justified in seeking a lower total settlement package, since money that you have in your possession today tends to have a greater value than the promise of money down the line. At the same time, you and your attorney might feel that it is more desirable to accept a lower total package in favor of the security of not having to wait and wonder if the maintenance and support payments are going to be there every month for years to come.

However you balance your particular financial equation, it is essential that you base your decisions on the realities of your specific situation. Perhaps most importantly, you and your estranged spouse owe it to yourselves—and particularly to your children—to hammer out solutions that will be satisfactory to all concerned.

Note

1. Block, Julian. *Julian Block's Year-Round Tax Strategies*. Rocklin, CA: Prima Publishing and Communications, 1990.

7

The Emotions of
Loving and Leaving

I n describing the intricacies of my profession, I have often
noted that a box of tissues is almost as essential in my day-to-
day work as my lawbooks. Please don't get me wrong. I'm not
trying to be glib about the trauma and turmoil couples undergoing divorce experience. It's just that I am acutely aware of how
traumatic a role emotions can play in the divorce process. Indeed, they frequently overshadow all other factors.

If a married couple were encountering some emotional
problems, they could go for counseling and attempt to resolve
these difficulties. At that point, the spouses and their counselor
would be dealing strictly on the emotional level—and that's complex enough.

Once the decision to divorce has been made, however, the
whole package becomes infinitely more complicated. There's the
financial turmoil, the effect on children and other family members—not to speak of all the complications pertaining to lawyers
and the court system. While you are desperately trying to keep
afloat in these turbulent crosscurrents, you are simultaneously
experiencing a profound emotional trauma.

I mentioned earlier that divorce is often cited as the second
most traumatic experience in life. Researchers have found that
only the death of a loved one is worse. My personal belief is that,
in many instances, divorce can be far more upsetting than the
death of someone close.

At least, the physical death of a loved one is final. As difficult
as it may be to face that reality, most of us eventually come to

accept the impossibility of bringing back our dearly departed. Thus, we accept the natural order of things, and go ahead with our lives.

When you divorce, it is often far more difficult to attain that same sense of acceptance and closure. One lives with the nagging thought that the estranged person is still around. In a very real sense, he or she is just a phone call away. Such thoughts can provide fertile soil in which preexisting emotional attachments can linger on.

There is often a sense of longing, the wish that things could return to the way they once were. Even clients who have been divorced for years have told me that they sometimes wake up in the middle of the night, haunted by one or more of the following unsettling thoughts:

- Maybe I made a mistake.
- What did I do wrong?
- I should have found a way to keep my marriage together.
- I've done irreparable harm to my children.
- My life will never again be what it once was.

I asked Dr. Naomi Leiter, a respected New York psychiatrist, herself a survivor of divorce trauma, how long it takes for most people to overcome those intense feelings of grief and remorse. Let me share her thoughts with you:

"My experience is that it often takes people at least two years to get over the immediate trauma of divorce, and five years total to ride out the experience.

"Once all the papers are signed, you can expect it to take another three years to get your life together. At that point, you can finally tell yourself: 'It's finished—it's over.' Of course, some people need less time to recover. On the other hand, there are others who are riddled with guilt and regret ten or even twenty years later.

"In general, you have to differentiate between divorcing couples who have children and those who are childless. You're facing a far more difficult and complicated situation when there are children involved—especially young children. Nevertheless, even childless couples, or those with grown children, have to accept certain stark realities.

"You've lost a friend—someone with whom you were once extremely close. That person supported you and shared your most intimate thoughts and dreams. But now the relationship is over. Many people find it takes a very long time for that reality to sink in. In the meantime, they have to live with a tremendous amount of ambivalence.

"Before this experience can be put to rest, most people have to go through a period of mourning. You'll be upset. You'll be afraid. But if you can find the strength to start over again, it may all be worth it."

Should You Stay or Should You Go?

As I told you in the opening chapter, one of the first questions I almost always ask clients is, "Can your marriage be saved?" If there is even the slightest possibility of a reconciliation, I encourage the person to seek marriage counseling before proceeding with the divorce.

I realize that many people are skeptical about attorneys—and perhaps rightfully so. Obviously, a lawyer won't make very much money if he successfully convinces every new client to seek counseling and avoid divorce. Nevertheless, I would be thrilled if most of the potential divorce clients could repair their marriages.

I like to think of myself as a human being first and an attorney second. If there was any way to quell the human suffering I've witnessed on the front lines of the divorce wars, no sacrifice would be too great. Unfortunately, the widespread suffering is not going to abate until human nature is elevated to a place where rationality outweighs the need for revenge and retribution.

If we were sitting face-to-face, I'd try to evaluate your particular situation, and together we would formulate an appropriate plan of action. As it is, we have to consider these matters from a somewhat more general point of view. Although this book is not meant to be a substitute for consulting with an experienced attorney or therapist, it gives you an opportunity to evaluate your options and start making positive and productive decisions.

Before we go any further, I'd like you to take a moment to get in touch with where you are in terms of marriage and divorce. Take a few minutes to look over the brief statements in the following exercise. Then put a check next to each statement that describes your situation. I have also left room for you to add some descriptive statements of your own.

WHICH OF THESE STATEMENTS DESCRIBES YOU?

- I am thinking about leaving my spouse.
- My spouse has informed me that he/she plans to leave me.
- I have already left my spouse—we are now living apart.
- My spouse has already left me—we are now living apart.
- My spouse and I have agreed to divorce.
- My spouse and I have gone to marriage counseling, and it was mutually decided that it would be in our best interest to end the marriage.
- My spouse and I have never sought marriage counseling.
- I have suggested marriage counseling, but he/she says it is too late.
- My spouse has suggested marriage counseling, but I say it is too late.
- The primary reason for this marriage ending is an overall lack of communication.
- The primary reason for this marriage ending is that my spouse and I were a bad match in the first place.
- I feel that it's too late for my spouse and me to work things out, but I would consider individual counseling or short-term psychotherapy for the sake of my own personal growth.
- I consider myself to be the rejecting spouse.
- I consider myself to be the rejected spouse.
- I'm leaning toward divorce, but I feel ambivalent because of the children.

- I am concerned about the effect divorce would have on my friends and family.
- I feel I've been greatly wronged by my spouse, and I want to get even.
- The impetus for my wanting to end this marriage is another man/woman.
- The impetus for my spouse wanting to end this marriage is another man/woman.
- I have had one or more affairs in the course of my marriage.
- My spouse has had one or more affairs in the course of our marriage.
-
-
-

Now that you've checked off the relevant statements in the above exercise, write down the ones that apply to you on a separate piece of paper. This simple step will help increase your awareness and give you a better sense of what needs to be done.

I am aware that divorce will turn out to be the best option for some of you. Nevertheless, before you make this monumental decision, I want you to give this matter all the consideration it deserves. Then, if you do decide to end the marriage, you will be in a far better position to use the experience to enhance—rather than destroy—your self-esteem. Let's take a moment to explore that concept.

I know that some of you may find it an old-fashioned notion, but we are living in a world that puts far greater value on external satisfaction than on personal growth. When we look at the advertisements on television and in magazines, we see a world of glamour, fascinating people, and erotic sex. How much more exotic this is than our humdrum lives! We all have insecurities and are, therefore, vulnerable to such enticements. When there are problems in our marriage, it's much easier to look at that terrific world that awaits us out there—if only we could get rid of that albatross around our neck.

On the other hand, think of all the time you've spent laying a foundation for your relationship. You might find electricity and excitement with someone new, but it's going to take many years to lay the same kind of groundwork that now exists between you and your current spouse.

If you feel that your marriage is deteriorating, don't just give up. Talk to your spouse. If that's too hard, try sending a letter. Perhaps you can suggest marriage counseling as a possible way to better your marriage. In any case, don't just walk out without adequately exploring other options.

When you think about the potential damage a divorce can have on you—not to speak of your spouse and children—don't you owe it to yourself to at least consider the possibility of trying to work things out?

Dr. Sylvan Schaffer is a noted Manhattan clinical psychologist who is also an attorney. As someone who has witnessed the divorce process from a wide perspective, he feels strongly that too many couples cut and run without even considering reparative measures.

"The first thing the couple should do is decide if they really need to get divorced," counsels Dr. Schaffer. "You look at some people who are divorcing and say, 'Why are they doing this to themselves?' Many times there may not be a really valid reason.

"Perhaps they were experiencing some problems and just never looked into any options for solving them. Rather than running to a divorce lawyer, many couples would be far better off discussing their difficulties with a marriage counselor. Perhaps with some conscious effort and a little work, they could make themselves into partners who can live together.

"Sometimes marital problems can be relatively minor. If these difficulties are dealt with soon enough, divorce can often be avoided. In order to make a marriage work, people have to be adaptable, flexible, and willing to compromise. But it takes a certain amount of courage to face your problems and try to do something about them."

Dr. Schaffer points out that people who cut and run from one marriage are likely to take the same easy way out in future relationships. For the most part, I share that view.

We have become a society obsessed with instant gratification. Why work at improving a relationship in which we've invested so much time and effort when it's so much easier to just walk out? The answer is, of course, that the cut-and-run approach may be expedient, but in the long run, it's often not the best solution.

When a couple has children, they are often more likely to seek out counseling—or at least to think twice—before simply walking out of a marriage. But for childless couples, it's a far simpler matter to cut their losses and split—particularly when both spouses have careers.

For a relatively young, two-career, childless couple that has been married less than five years, the process of uncoupling is becoming increasingly simpler. A growing number of states (including California, Connecticut, and Ohio) have adopted *summary dissolution laws*. In those states, you can simply fill out the necessary forms in front of a court clerk, and shortly thereafter, you're divorced.

While *summary dissolution laws* generally come into play when a couple has few substantial assets, even wealthier couples without children often find it relatively easy to dissolve a marriage. Because more women are delaying child rearing in favor of establishing careers, I've been handling a lot more of what I've come to call "yuppie" (young urban professional) or "dink" (double-income, no kids) divorces.

Assuming that such a couple isn't determined to wage a full-scale war and that their attorneys are reasonable, hammering out the terms of divorce can be a comparatively straightforward process.

Nevertheless, we come back to our original question: Should you stay or should you go? Is it desirable to leave a marriage just because there are a few apparent impediments, or is it wiser to stick around and try to work things out?

We've explored some reasons for keeping your marriage going. Let's now examine the other side of that coin. There are no meaningful statistics that tell us how many broken marriages could have been saved by a little more effort on the part of the spouses. At the same time, who can say how many unhappily married couples would, ultimately, be better off if they opted for divorce?

"When I first started out in psychiatry," says Dr. Naomi Leiter, "I used to think that people should get into counseling or therapy and do everything they could to work things out. But in recent years, I have changed my point of view regarding divorce, as well as the entire concept of working things through.

"Sometimes it's better for people to just accept that a relationship is finished. If, for example, you've been married for three years, and you've been having ongoing problems that three different counselors or therapists couldn't help you resolve, a pretty good case can be made for cutting your losses.

"There is the old-fashioned idea that we have to work hard at our relationships, and I certainly can see the value in that. Still, if the core of a relationship is good, there should be a certain natural flow—particularly in the first few years.

"A fundamentally good relationship should not require an inordinate amount of effort. Of course, all couples have certain problems and differences that can be worked out—either by developing better communication skills or through counseling. Still, if a certain basic compatibility isn't there, you may not be able to solve the problems, no matter how hard you work.

"As much as I'm in favor of marriage as an institution, I've seen some couples work so hard at making their relationship work, it sapped all their energy and left them emotionally spent. Many of them were afraid that giving up would be an admission of failure. In a sense, there's a certain amount of truth in that. Nevertheless, there comes a time where an amicable divorce is preferable to a miserable marriage.

"It's tough watching a couple dragging a bad relationship on and on, without making any real inroads. Just as a surgeon sometimes has to advise a patient that it's necessary to amputate a gangrenous limb, I periodically have to counsel clients that severing a bad relationship may, in the long run, be in their best interests."

Now that we've explored both sides of the argument, we are still left with a problem that does not lend itself to easy resolution. With all that's involved, how do you decide whether or not to stay together? I certainly hope you will take my advice, and not just cut out without at least considering counseling and other reparative measures.

My basic instinct is to tell you that if you're still hedging about what to do, try to hang in and work things out. Still, as I look around at my friends and business associates, I can see the whole spectrum of problems and answers.

Some of them have successful long-term marriages. Some of them are divorced and happily remarried. Some are divorced and miserably lonely. Some have substantial marital problems but are sticking it out—ostensibly for the sake of the children. Some have never been married. Still others are divorced and are in the process of reconciling with their ex-spouses.

It seems to me that, in general, the people I know who are married are happier than those who are divorced or single. Indeed, many mental health professionals indicate that marriage has a beneficial effect on one's emotional, and even physical, health.

In the end, the decision about whether to stay or leave a marriage is in your hands. After all, even the best counselor or therapist can't know as much about your marriage as you do.

If I had to draw a general conclusion, it would be that people who go to counseling, learn to understand their problems, and carefully consider their options are far better off than those who leap before they look. Unless your divorce can serve as a foundation for future growth and increased self-esteem, I believe that you are better off holding onto your present marriage.

Understanding the Dynamics Behind the Psychological Divorce

Whether or not you've made the final decision to divorce or are just considering it, it's important to understand something about the forces that have pulled (or are pulling) you and your spouse apart. But first I'd like you to take a few moments to look over the following checklist.

I've listed some of the reasons that are most frequently given when people are asked why they are getting divorced. Put a check to the left of each statement that is relevant to your particular situation. There is also space provided for you to write in any other statements or feelings that you might have on this matter.

Why Are You Divorcing?

- The marriage was a mistake in the first place. We're simply not right for each other.
- We fight and argue all the time.
- We no longer share the same values and interests.
- I feel unappreciated and misunderstood.
- We haven't been able to communicate in a long time.
- I'm not making my spouse happy. We'd be better off apart.
- I can no longer tolerate my spouse's (list his/her three most abrasive qualities).
- My spouse is so involved in his/her career, we're not really together anyway.
- Our sex life was once terrific, but now it's almost nonexistent.
- I'm having an affair with someone else and want to be with him/her.
- My spouse is having an affair with someone else and now wants to be with him/her.
- I'm not that unhappy with the relationship, but my spouse has made it clear that he/she no longer loves me, and wants out of the marriage.
-
-
-

Before we discuss some of the other key issues raised in the checklist, I want to ask you an important question that underlies some of the above statements:

Are You the Rejector or the Rejectee?

We've already touched on some of the differences between the person initiating the divorce and the spouse who finds himself or herself on the receiving end of the news. While there are some instances in which couples make a mutual decision to divorce— often with the help of a therapist or counselor—such cases are all too rare.

In the great majority of broken marriages, there is a rejector and a rejectee. Depending on your position, you're likely to be facing a particular set of emotional difficulties. I've asked Dr. Leiter to share her insights on this critical psychological question.

"The person who has presumably been deserted (the rejectee) is in a totally different position from the one who is leaving (the rejector).

"The rejectee is forced to deal with feelings of abandonment, depression, and loss. Suddenly, he or she finds it nearly impossible not to be overwhelmed by the following emotions:

- Confusion: Why is this happening to me?
- Guilt: What did I do wrong?
- Insecurity: How am I going to make it on my own?
- Self-doubt: Why do bad things always happen to me?
- Revenge: What can I do to get back at ____?

"Rejected spouses have to allow themselves to get in touch with these feelings before they can resolve them. It's going to take some time, but you will be able to pick up the pieces of your life. First, however, you have to go through certain steps.

Face the Reality of What Has Happened to You. There is no way to reconstruct the past. Whatever it is that is being done to you is now a fact of life.

Pick Up from There. Once you accept the fact that being rejected is not the end of the world, you must begin living in the present and start rebuilding your life.

Stop Seeing Yourself as a Victim. It's self-defeating and untrue that being a rejectee marks you as a loser. Under the circumstances, it's tempting to indulge in self-pity, but this will only lengthen the process of renewal.

Take Control of Your Life and Go On. Each of us has only so much time on this planet, and we owe it to ourselves to pursue happiness and self-fulfillment. Many former rejectees have rebuilt their lives and are now far better off than they were before their divorce. My own experience may be instructive.

"I was the spouse who was left—the rejectee. After seventeen years of marriage, my husband left me for another woman. I wasn't making much money because I was only working part-time. Although I had custody of our two young children, I suddenly had to find full-time work in order to support them.

"From a financial point of view, I guess I was luckier than a lot of women. You might think that because I am a psychiatrist, I wouldn't have been as quite as vulnerable—you're wrong—I was devastated. Until I went through it myself, I was quite naive about how traumatic divorce could be.

"Basically, I was a typical rejectee. I believed that my ex-spouse was correct in his assessment that I was crazy, stupid, unattractive—and unworthy of his love after seventeen years of marriage.

"I also had to face the fact that I hadn't been happy with the marriage for some time. Once I started to collect myself, I was able to look at the relationship in more objective terms. At one point, I realized that life with this guy was pretty bad. I had to ask myself: How much worse could it be without him?

"I struggled long and hard to reconstruct my life. And now, fourteen years later, I am much more successful professionally, far happier in my personal relationship, and infinitely more fulfilled sexually. Nevertheless, the pain can last for many years.

"Recently, I woke up feeling kind of bad about some things in my children's lives. It saddened me that I did not have a chance to be as good a mother as I wanted to be through some of their significant years because I was depressed and driven by the need to support them financially.

"Looking back on it now, there really wasn't much else I could do. Overall, being rejected by my husband was probably the best thing that could have happened. But there is still some lingering sadness—particularly in relation to the children."

While Dr. Leiter admits to being more empathetic toward the rejectee, she is, nevertheless, fully aware of the rejector's position.

"The person doing the rejecting has a tremendous amount of control—even though he or she might not see it in that light. In making a unilateral decision to leave, the rejector has had ample opportunity to deal with any negative feelings. People in this position often feel guilt, but they can handle it in their own good time.

"As a rule, divorce is much easier on rejectors. The spouse in this position often has another lover whom he or she has been seeing for some time. Except for any guilt, remorse, or concern about the financial settlement, rejectors often feel very good about the new direction in which their lives are going.

"On the other hand, I've seen rejectors go through mood swings that are almost manic-depressive in nature. On the up side, they are having an affair with somebody. That can make a person feel excited and elated. At the same time, breaking up a family and going through a divorce is never easy—not even for the rejector. People in this position shouldn't allow themselves to become too manic, or they might be in for trouble when it's time to receive the depressive goods that are an inevitable part of the divorce package.

"Actually I've seen rejectors become quite depressed over their divorces. That's ironic, because the person is often in far greater command of their ship than he or she thinks. The bottom line is: although people on both sides of the fence can become anxious or depressed, divorce is usually less traumatic for the person who makes the decision to leave."

While I agree with Dr. Leiter's perception about the relative positions of the rejector and the rejectee, I feel that rejectors have to be careful not to let their feelings of guilt undermine them.

One approach that you may want to consider is divorce counseling. Together with a counselor, you and your spouse can begin hammering out the nonfinancial terms of a reasonable and, hopefully, amicable split. This approach gives the rejected partner an opportunity to be a collaborator in the decision-making process. He or she is less apt to feel like a victim, while you will be far less riddled with guilt and remorse. We'll talk about divorce counseling in more detail on page 119.

Extramarital Affairs, Sex, and Divorce

One of the first questions people are tempted to ask a man or woman who is initiating a divorce is: "Are you having an affair?" It has been variously estimated that 35 to 70 percent of husbands and 20 to 50 percent of wives have at least one affair in the course of their marriage.

Since people are not always forthcoming about these matters, I tend to be somewhat skeptical about such statistics. Nevertheless, there is no question that the issues of sex and sexual cheating are key to understanding the emotions of divorce.

An observer from a more high-minded universe might wonder why husbands and wives cheat on one another. Do we not make a commitment to be faithful to our spouse? By having an affair, don't we violate that pledge and, thus, make a choice that diminishes us even in our own eyes?

Unfortunately, in this world, the human psyche is often a bit less than staunch. When we have problems, we tend to look for the easy way out. Thus, if things aren't going well between you and your spouse, why try to make the situation better when it's easier to find what you need outside the marriage?

One only need watch television or open a magazine to see the shallowness of the messages our culture gives us regarding sex. How can a wife compete with that sex goddess up there on the screen? How can a husband compete with the hunk of a pop singer?

The answer is that no flesh-and-blood human being can compete. Even if he or she actually was more beautiful or sexier than that image on the screen, it would be very difficult for the spouses to perceive them in that way.

There is something about human nature that makes what we don't have appear to be much more desirable than that which is readily available to us. I refer to this as the "grass-is-greener syndrome." It is my perception that many people who seek out extramarital affairs are not so much looking for someone better, rather they are looking for someone new and different.

At one point your spouse, too, was new and exciting. But as a married couple falls into the routine of daily living, it's difficult to maintain that initial chemistry or electricity. People will complain that they're bored. But herein lies a basic misunderstanding of what marriage is about. What can be negatively perceived as boredom can also be understood as the kind of comfort and warmth that are so essential in ongoing relationships.

Please keep in mind that your new affair will be subject to the same rules of atrophy that dimmed the flame between you and your spouse. One day, your new lover will also be boringly familiar—that is, if you stay together long enough. Then you'll be right back where you started.

It is not my intention to moralize, but I happen to be a great believer in the old-fashioned notion of monogamous marriage. Instead of discarding what you have, maybe you'd be better off trying to improve your current sexual relationship—even if it means seeking counseling or therapy.

I've observed that many people who have extramarital affairs do so to abate loneliness or to lift a sagging ego. At the same time, there is also a feeling that you are getting away with something when you cheat. This may give you a bit of a momentary thrill, but think of the potential cost in terms of your credibility and self-esteem. If you eventually decide to marry your lover, why should he or she believe your vow to be faithful? In fact, why should you believe yourself?

While there are some sound arguments against extramarital affairs, I fully expect that some of you will plunge right into them anyway. Furthermore, others of you are undoubtedly in the midst of an affair even as you read this. In any case, I don't believe that having an affair is, in and of itself, a good enough reason for divorce.

Most of the mental health professionals I've spoken with share this point of view. Furthermore, if statistics on the number of people who cheat on their spouses is anywhere close to being accurate, there would be precious few marriages left if the spouse of every person who had an affair did seek a divorce.

"If you are going into an extramarital relationship," observes Dr. Leiter, "I can only offer two rather pointed observations: 1) There's going to be trouble, and 2) You'd better take it as a warning sign that something is wrong in the marriage.

"I have always believed that unsatisfactory sex is the underlying cause of many divorces. Therefore, when a patient suddenly tells me that he or she wants a divorce, I am immediately suspicious that an extramarital affair is the motivating force. This is just a gut feeling—but more often than not I am right.

"When somebody announces that they want out of a marriage, my first question is: 'Are you sleeping with somebody else?' Their answers might not necessarily be 'yes,' but that person still might be having an affair.

"If someone has already decided to end the marriage, an affair can be a useful catalyst for the rejecting spouse. But if the idea is to keep the marriage together, the person must either be willing to give up the extramarital relationship, or at least admit that it exists.

"In this day and age, I don't think most spouses would walk out of a marriage just because their partner was having an affair. But again, I find that men and women who are reasonably satisfied with their partners do not usually seek out an extramarital relationship. Furthermore, it is my experience that people who are sexually happy with their spouses rarely get divorced.

"From my perspective, an affair is not something a married person should ever go into lightly. In fact, even the desire for an extramarital affair should be taken as a sign of trouble in a marriage.

"More and more, I am encountering men and women who are not sexually happy. Female patients admit that they are feigning orgasms—and their husbands do not know it. Many husbands are also less than forthcoming with their wives about these matters. But when two people are truly sexually satisfied—and satisfying to each other—they are far less likely to split up.

"The same principle applies to a marriage. If you like each other sexually and physically, if there's communication and emotional warmth, if you share similar interests and mutual friends, you're likely to stay together. Naturally, there are things to work out in all these areas—and sex is no exception.

"A man may like making love in the morning, while his wife may prefer the night. After the lovemaking is finished, a woman may want to be held, while her husband may want to turn over and sack out. All these differences can be resolved if couples learn to adapt and try to have fun with one another. If you can't do this on your own, counseling or therapy can be very helpful."

I fully agree with Dr. Leiter that couples can do a great deal to resolve their sexual difficulties—without resorting to cheating. This extra effort is especially warranted if you and your spouse have children, since they are the ones who often suffer the most damage when one or both parents have extramarital affairs.

If for no other reason, the potential impact of divorce on children makes it is impossible to broach the issue of marital sex without at least touching on the question of personal ethics. I realize that this is a concern that is not very fashionable in the 1990s. Nevertheless, certain consequences result from the choices you make.

If you are honest and play it straight with the people in your life, you set yourself up to win, in the best sense of the term. When you lie and deceive the person you have vowed to honor and cherish, you have chosen a course of action that can only result in feelings of guilt and diminished self-esteem. Whether or not you ultimately stay with your spouse, these negative feelings only can affect you adversely.

Man vs. Woman: Two Different Perspectives on Loving and Leaving

In discussing the role of sex in the emotional divorce, it is important to differentiate between the male and female perspectives—though the same may be said for any number of issues that enter into the picture.

Several years ago, there was an article in the *New York Times* that went so far as to conclude that every marriage was, in fact, two marriages—his and hers.[1] If that is indeed the case, divorce must also be viewed in the same light.

The forces that make a marriage work are a mirror image of those that cause a marriage to fail. Therefore, if good communication is the key to a viable marriage, it follows that a lack of communication is nothing less than a formula for divorce.

But where ought we place the bulk of the blame—on men or women? Dr. Sylvan Schaffer believes that it cuts both ways:

"There are so many reasons why people get divorced," notes Dr. Schaffer. "You can hardly attribute it to any one cause—much less to any one gender.

"Some people find another lover and initiate a divorce. Some couples simply drift apart and mutually agree to end the relationship. Very young people often marry without really evaluating what they are doing. In some cases, the woman gets pregnant and the couple marries out of a sense of obligation. These are scenarios that often result in divorce.

"Actually, there are all sorts of reasons why marriages break up that are, more or less, gender-neutral. For example, I've seen many couples who were incapable of living with each other because one or both have severe emotional problems. Then, of course, there are often major differences relating to values and goals.

"You don't have to feel the same about everything, but there does need to be a certain meeting of the minds on critical issues. For example, if one spouse wants to have children, and the other is dead set against it, there can be major problems. If you leave something like that unresolved indefinitely, you're eventually going to need an attorney.

"I've seen many people break up because of a basic incompatibility that has festered for many years. Some couples fight a lot, and that's okay if they can kiss and make up. But others marry without considering what their lives are going to be like, only to find that they have very little in common.

"I'm not saying that a married couple has to have identical

values and interests, but there has to be a basic compatibility. If the husband says, 'I'm hooked on sports. I'm going to plop down every weekend in front of that TV, so don't call me for forty-eight hours,' while the wife wants to go out and do things with friends, you have the beginning of a potentially serious problem.

"I've seen other couples have trouble because one spouse likes to be alone and the other needs constant companionship. If couples want to avoid the kinds of resentment and frustration that lead to divorce, they have to decide whether they're people-people, career-people, stay-at-home people, go-out-a-lot people. Those are the kinds of things a couple has to start analyzing early on if they want to avoid divorce."

Like Dr. Schaffer, I have worked with clients who divorce for myriad reasons. Nevertheless, I am finding that the driving force behind more and more broken marriages is the disparity between male and female expectations, and the resulting lack of communication.

I find that women are far more in touch with their need for emotional intimacy and are thus more willing to face marital difficulties. In general, women have a greater ability to accept the pain of marital introspection, and more of a capacity to understand and rectify differences.

On the other hand, most of my male clients tend to avoid and shy away from introspection about marital difficulties. As much as possible, they depersonalize, externalize, and avoid confrontations with their wives. Too many men approach their marital difficulties like ostriches. They either bury their heads, spread their plumage to mate with another, or do both. Let's look at some of the reasons behind these differences.

The working man in the traditional one-income household is often exhausted at the end of the day. He feels that he has fulfilled his role by working hard and providing a secure, comfortable home. Basically, he wants to be left alone. If he comes home to a clean house and a hot dinner, this type of husband is relatively content to tune out in front of the television—and occasionally make love to his wife.

Now, a wife in this kind of marriage may tolerate such an arrangement for a time. But, by and large, she is unhappy. Because of her greater need for emotional intimacy, she wants to talk things over—especially problems of the children and other matters pertaining to the relationship.

Unfortunately, her husband has put the bulk of his emotional energy into his work. While his wife may perceive a discussion—or even an argument—about problems and difficulties as a way to increase intimacy, he sees it as an intrusion on his peace and quiet.

Of course, most relationships don't start out that way. As Ted Huston, a psychologist at the University of Texas at Austin who has done extensive research in this area, notes:

"During courtship, men are more than willing to talk to a woman in ways that enhance feelings of intimacy. But after marriage, husbands tend to spend less and less time talking to their wives in these ways. Instead, they seem more eager to expend their emotional energy on work or male friends.

"This kind of long-term diminution of interest is bound to have an adverse effect on the marriage—particularly from the woman's point-of-view."[2]

I believe these differences in expectations also express themselves in the different way men and women respond to marital adversity. Aside from tuning out, men often display their dissatisfaction by engaging in extramarital sex. However, a good number of these same men would not necessarily admit that substantial problems existed in the marriage.

More and more, it is women, particularly those over the age of thirty, who are initiating divorces—despite statistics that indicate that they suffer more financially than do men.

The case of Sam, a successful business manager, is somewhat prototypical of older couples who divorce. Sam is fifty-six years old and has been married to his wife, Helen, for thirty years. The marriage has produced two children, both of whom are now married with families of their own. It's been about a year since Helen left Sam, and he is emotionally devastated.

I happen to be the husband's attorney in this particular divorce, so believe me when I tell you that there's no bitterness between the parties—no scorched-earth or World-War-III tactics. Quite the contrary: Sam and Helen are still friends. Ironically, this lack of anger and hostility is one of the things my client finds most difficult.

"Bernie," he says plaintively. "I don't understand why she

left. I did everything I thought I was supposed to do. I worked hard to become a successful businessman, and I have always been a good provider. I gave her everything: a beautiful home, expensive vacations—anything she wanted.

"Beyond that, we rarely fought with each other. I was completely faithful. Never even looked at another woman in thirty years of marriage. Never drank or gambled. It's true that my work required long hours and a great deal of dedication, but I was doing it as much for Helen and the kids as for myself."

Helen's desire to end the marriage, was, apparently, driven by the kind of long-term dissatisfaction that comes when one's emotional needs are not being met. She freely expresses appreciation for the economic affluence that Sam provided, and is not looking for an unreasonable financial settlement. But clearly she wants out of the marriage.

Beyond unmet emotional expectations, there really is no practical need for Helen to leave. Yes, her children are on their own, and there is a temptation to flee an empty nest. Still, as Sam points out, "There's nothing so terrific waiting for her out there."

Helen herself acknowledges this reality. At fifty-three, she is not overly optimistic about remarrying. Having been a housewife for the past thirty years, she's not quite sure what she's going to do with her time. Still, she feels that she has been stifled as a person for all these years, and now she wants the opportunity to see what she can make of her life—one that doesn't include Sam.

Shortly after the proceedings started, Sam related a story to me. He ran into his wife's brother, with whom he has had a cordial relationship. "I don't understand it," Sam plaintively remarked to his brother-in-law. "I'm not asking you to reveal any confidences. But please, tell me what I did wrong. What's the complaint?"

He said: "Sam, your wife has nothing bad to say about you. In fact, she acknowledges that you didn't do anything that most typical businessman husbands haven't done. You were loyal, hard-working, had peer acceptance, and were a good provider. Your only crime was that you never gave Helen the sensitivity and emotional support that she needed."

In essence, Sam did what he had always been programmed

to do. He was taught that to be a successful businessman you had to bust your butt. And that's exactly what he did. Unfortunately, he never took the time to notice that he had put all his emotions into his profession—at the expense of his marriage. As he himself now realizes:

"When I came home at night, I was so tired that all I wanted to do was relax. I work in a high-pressure field where every day is a battle. Negotiations. Deals. Yelling. Tensions. The constant pressure mounts up. By the time you come home, there's not a lot of emotion left for anything too dramatic."

To my mind, one unfortunate aspect of this case is that Sam is so thoroughly enmeshed in this all-American image of a good husband, he can't really see how he could have done it any differently. Instead of looking inward, Sam tends to blame external forces. As he recently remarked:

"I think the women's lib movement is largely responsible for this phenomenon of women pulling out of marriages. Today's woman reads so much crap in the literature, she has developed unrealistic expectations of what is out there.

"It seems to me that many women are looking for one external orgasm—in an emotional sense. I think my wife is going to be very disappointed when she finds out that nothing like that exists, at least not in this world. I wish she could just accept that real happiness comes from within. To me, there's nothing so terribly wrong with the life we had."

Under the circumstances, I suppose a certain amount of sour grapes is understandable. Still, since Sam's complaint about the women's movement is not atypical, I thought it would be helpful to get Dr. Naomi Leiter's input on this matter.

"In general, I'm very much in favor of women's liberation. I think it's great that women are taking more responsibility for their lives—both financially and emotionally. It's also good to see women being more supportive of one another, and feeling better about themselves—professionally, as parents, and as spouses.

"At the same time, women's liberation is also having an effect on the role of men. Husbands are becoming more involved in taking care of the home, changing diapers, and sharing in the cooking. Hopefully, these shifting and overlapping roles will make men and women more sensitive to one another.

"While I'm confident that these changes will be positive in the long run, there are aspects that worry me in cases like that of Sam and Helen.

"I think it's dangerous for a person to give something up without having anything else to take its place. That's why I don't suggest leaving a marriage unless you are sure that there is something to replace it.

"I'm all for getting in touch with your needs and taking control of your life. Just make sure that you don't leave until there is some kind of plan or support system in place to fill the gap."

I understand that Helen is having some problems in this area; however, she is coping, and it is doubtful that she will want to reconcile with her estranged husband. To his credit, Sam is trying his best to hold up. Not surprisingly, he is drowning himself in work, but lately, he is starting to better understand that, relative to himself, his wife is coming from a completely different emotional point of view. In essence, they were two trains traveling only on parallel tracks and never meeting for most of the past thirty years. Nevertheless, Sam still has a good deal of guilt and remorse to work through before he can put this behind him.

"I feel an enormous sense of personal failure," he recently confided, "and also a great deal of sadness. My wife says this is my fault. That I didn't react to the messages she was sending to me all along. Apparently, she was crying out for a lot more interfacing, emotional support, caring, and intimacy than I was able to give. That's why she says she was forced to leave the marriage. I'm starting to think that maybe she is right."

Personally, I don't feel there is much to be gained by characterizing the expectations of either gender as inherently good or bad. To some degree, it may be possible that these emotional predispositions are biologically determined. To a much greater extent, they have been shaped by traditional social roles.

Even in the best marriages, men and women are bound to have different expectations; however, if they are seen in the right context, such differences don't have to be divisive or destructive. In any case, it is unlikely that these basic gender-related characteristics will change any time soon. Nevertheless, greater understanding can be achieved through communication—and, perhaps, a bit of humor, on both sides. This harks back to the concept of avoiding divorce by working a little harder at marriage.

Unfortunately, too many people make the same mistake as Sam and Helen. Perhaps Helen could have tried a little harder to make Sam more aware of her needs. And maybe if Sam would have been a little less married to his career, he would have sensed that there were problems festering. Now that they are apart, Helen and Sam find it relatively easy to be forthcoming about their differences. But the real question is: Why didn't they try harder to talk about their problems while the marriage was still viable?

Some Suggestions for a Less Emotionally Traumatic Divorce

The intensity of the divorce trauma depends to a great extent on how much effort two people have put into making the marriage viable. If you tried your best to work things out, you probably won't feel as devastated if you and your spouse ultimately split up.

Here again, we come back to the idea that many of our emotional problems are based on feelings of low self-esteem. Divorce may cause a great upheaval in your life, but it certainly doesn't have to be a source of shame.

Some divorced people find that certain friends no longer want to see them. Women, in particular, have complained of this problem. "It's as if I have some kind of disease that my married girlfriends think is contagious," one female client confided. "I don't know, maybe they're also a little worried that I'll go after their husbands."

Divorce can certainly be an isolating experience—at least initially. In time, however, you will make new friends. Remember, there are plenty of men and women out there who are in the same boat. Still, perhaps you've conducted yourself in ways that you now feel badly about. If so, you simply have to learn from your mistakes and try to do better in the future. One of the first steps in renewal is forgiving yourself—and others—for past transgressions. Some people can do this on their own. Others may need the help and support of a counselor or therapist.

Ultimately, there is no magic pill or quick fix for abating the emotional nightmare of divorce. If anything, it usually requires a long and arduous healing process.

It is ironic that the key to winning at divorce involves taking control of our destinies. It is not, however, easy to be reasonable and rational when your emotional identity is being threatened. Still, in the final analysis, there is no other way.

We've talked a great deal in this chapter about the value of counseling and therapy. As I pointed out earlier, seeking professional help should be viewed as a sign of strength, not weakness. But herein lies still another irony.

When you are going through a heavy emotional crisis and turn to a mental health professional for help, it's only natural to want and expect that person to take control of your life. After all, since these services cost a good deal of money, the least you can expect is someone to help you shoulder the emotional burden.

Here again, we come back to the concept of captain and navigator. You are the only one who can make decisions about your life. A therapist can help clarify your options and put you more in touch with your goals. He or she can help you work out a road map so that it will be easier to proceed, but in the end, the final choices are yours.

Assuming that you have made the decision to divorce, there are ways to minimize the damage. One interesting way to achieve an amicable arrangement is through a collaborative process such as divorce counseling. Dr. Sylvan Schaffer explains how this process works:

"Assuming that two people have decided civilly that they want to end their marriage, it is possible to sit down with a counselor or therapist and evaluate their options. Obviously, if two people are completely hostile and are throwing things at one another, this approach isn't going to work. But there are many couples who simply have decided that their marriage is over. Such couples can approach their divorce in a collaborative way.

"In divorce therapy, the counselor or therapist helps the couple deal with their emotions so that they do not impede other aspects of the divorce process. This approach also helps people deal with the intricacies of the financial and legal arrangements.

"The good thing about divorce therapy is that it is a holistic process in which a couple learns to understand the nonemotional realities of divorce. At the same time, they learn both to own and to control their feelings.

"For example, you may feel guilty, but that doesn't mean you have to overreact or do something self-destructive. Or you may feel hurt, but that doesn't mean you have to try to punish the other person.

"In divorce therapy, people learn to deal with the hurt and the guilt—and to separate those emotions from the realities that form the rest of their lives. Recognizing and accepting your emotions is a positive step, but reacting to them in certain ways can be harmful.

"You may be angry at your spouse and want to do something to punish him or her. In the short term, you'll have vented your emotions, but in the long run, that may not be in your best interests. Part of this process involves helping clients to recognize the difference between short- and long-term gains."

Dr. Schaffer points out that divorce counseling can be an outgrowth of marriage counseling, or a completely separate process. If you and your spouse have been in marriage counseling, you can use the same therapist or someone else for the divorce counseling.

What I like about this collaborative approach to divorce is that it can be used to solve practical problems—as well as having a therapeutic effect. If more spouses would recognize the benefits of cooperating, the whole dichotomy between rejector and rejectee would be less of a factor. Then, many nightmarish divorces would be far less traumatic.

When a divorcing husband and wife have an opportunity to consider their options jointly, the proceedings tend to be far less painful and destructive. This consideration is particularly important for couples with children because, even though the marriage may be over, they will remain permanent partners in parenting.

In general, I believe that many more divorcing men and women could relieve a great deal of the pain by seeking therapy or counseling. To me, this is a positive step that can help you emerge a winner—in the best sense of the term.

Dr. Schaffer agrees that seeking this kind of help, far from being a sign of weakness, is an indication of real strength.

"I find it ironic that the men and women who seek therapy are often far healthier than those who don't. People who can admit that they have a problem also feel they have it within them to change their lives.

"It seems strange that, in the 1990s, there still can be a negative connotation to seeking psychological help. Nevertheless, when counseling or therapy is suggested, there are people who will say, 'I can't do that. People will think I'm crazy.' Actually, the opposite is true. It's the people who won't admit their difficulties—or feel that they can't change them—who have a far greater problem.

"It takes a certain amount of health and insight to admit that you need help and to seek it. Initiating that kind of positive action indicates that you really do have the potential to take control of your life—and to win at divorce."

Notes

1. "Two Views of Marriage Explored" by Daniel Goleman, *New York Times* (April 1, 1986), Section C, Science Times, page 1.
2. *Ibid.*

8

Grounds for Divorce

I n many old movies, there is a scene that goes something like
this:

> *Unfaithful husband:* I'm in love with Agnes, my secretary. I want
> to divorce you and live with her.
> *Spiteful wife:* That's just too bad, but there's no way I'm going
> to let you get away that easily.
> *Unfaithful husband:* Oh yeah, just what do you think you can do
> to stop me?
> *Spiteful wife:* You can move out of here if you want—and shack
> up with your hussy. But you're not going to marry her, because
> I'll die before I let you have a divorce.

Not so long ago, scenarios like this were very common. In
order to obtain a divorce, one spouse had to establish fault on
the part of the other. Since *adultery* is one of the primary fault
grounds, the wife in the above situation had a strong basis for
seeking a divorce. The husband, on the other hand, had no legal
grounds upon which to seek a divorce, unless he could make his
case on other fault grounds.

In theory, state and federal laws are supposed to reflect the
will of the people (that means you and me). Based on the upheaval in our values during the past several decades, it is apparent that our collective will has shifted radically. It may seem like
an old-fashioned notion in the 1990s, but it was not long ago that
couples were not so quick to throw in the towel in the face of
marital difficulties.

Now, it behooves the state to do what it can to endorse and encourage the institution of marriage. Indeed, the viability of our society hinges on matrimony, procreation, and adequate child-care. Before the mid-1960s, it was thought that married couples—and especially children—were better off when families stayed together, even in a bad marriage. The prevailing thinking has shifted, however, to the concept that unhappily married couples, and their children, are ultimately better off if the spouses go their separate ways.

We are still in transition both in terms of our legal principles and our values. Nevertheless, the laws in many states have come a long way in terms of reflecting those changes in our collective thinking.

We have now reached a point where, in the great majority of states, a spouse can obtain a divorce without having to demonstrate any fault whatsoever. In practical terms, this means that if your spouse wants to end the marriage, all he or she has to do is to go in front of a judge and state that there are irreconcilable differences or that the marriage has broken down irretrievably. Then, perhaps after a short waiting period, a divorce will be granted.

As we will see, this *no-fault divorce* system is not without some faults of its own. Nevertheless, this stance by the state legislatures is reflective of a society that has undergone a "do-your-own-thing" decade, a "me-generation" decade, and the onset of "yuppiedom." Coupled with the decline in the numbers of those who practice formal religion and the replacement of the extended family by the nuclear family—not to speak of the radical changes in traditional sexual roles—the clear message to our courts and legislatures from our culture is: "Let people divorce on demand."

I don't want you to get the mistaken impression that the state legislatures are all that sensitive to social change. The unfortunate truth is that the adoption of *no-fault divorce* laws is, as much as anything else, a matter of expedience designed to keep court *dockets* moving and to prevent embittered spouses from badgering the courts with trials that revolve around marital blame.

While there is a clear trend toward *no-fault divorce*, fault grounds still play a major role in a number of states—including

New York. Let's now examine the differences between *fault states* and those that will grant a divorce virtually upon request.

Fault vs. No-fault Divorce

It might be instructive to view the differences in how two neighboring states approach divorce. Connecticut is typical of those states that employ the *no-fault divorce* method, while New York is characteristic of a *fault state*.

In Connecticut, you serve a *summons* and *complaint* saying in effect that there has been an irretrievable breakdown of the marriage. At that point, there is really little else that the other side can say or do. There may be other valid grounds for ending the marriage, but you are not obliged to show them. In effect, all you have to do is tell the judge that you are seeking a divorce, and he or she is essentially bound to act in a way that says, "Okay—if you want it, you've got it."

As we will see shortly, there are ways in *fault states* like New York to effect something close to a *no-fault divorce*. Furthermore, even in fault states, if two people agree to the divorce, there is no problem working out the legalities. Still, no matter how you look at it, New Yorkers who want to end their marriages cannot do so nearly as easily as their neighbors in Connecticut. This can be a real problem if, as in the example that opened this chapter, one of the spouses decides to resist the divorce.

Why, a rational person might wonder, would a husband or wife attempt to persist in a union when their partner wanted out? There are any number of answers to this question. Spite, as we saw in our opening dialogue, is one factor. Continued love for the rejecting spouse may also play a role. Anxiety about letting go and starting anew is another consideration. The desire to hang tough in order to extract a bigger piece of the economic pie or more favorable child-care privileges also can motivate a rejected spouse to impede a divorce action. Whatever the underlying reason, the moving party in states like New York is generally obliged to establish proof of fault. It simply is not enough to just walk into court and announce that you want a divorce.

One reason for the growing popularity of *no-fault divorce* is that it prevents the kind of chamber of horrors spouses can fall into if they happen to reside in a *fault state*. I've told you more than once how risky it is to wage a court battle. Let's look at the situation in which a New York resident named Jane found herself when she attempted to sue her husband Alex for divorce.

Jane was alleging *adultery* on Alex's part. Note that even in New York there is a conflict among courts located in different parts of the state as to whether you can have *discovery* about fault. Let's assume that Jane lives in Buffalo, New York, where such investigation is permitted. She had spent two years arguing the case, going through the cumbersome legal steps we will be exploring in the next chapter. These included *discovery*, oral *depositions,* and written *interrogatories,* and the resulting investigations and evaluations. After all that, Jane still did not have the *quantum of proof* necessary to show that there was adultery.

This was especially painful to Jane because one night she came home early from a business trip and actually caught Alex in the act of having sex with another woman. Obviously, Alex knew he had committed adultery, but he and his lover lied about the incident. Both attorneys suspected that Jane's allegations were true, and so did the judge.

Nevertheless, after spending two years of her precious time and the bulk of her life's savings, Jane could not obtain a divorce. Why? Because the judge felt compelled to conclude that Jane did not prove her allegations of adultery. He seemed to be looking at her apologetically as he made the somber announcement that her divorce had been denied.

Such an outcome would make anyone feel bad enough. But imagine how much worse it would hurt knowing that if you were facing the same set of circumstances as a resident of an adjoining state, all you would have to do is express your desire to end the marriage. And presto, change! Through the magic of *no-fault divorce,* your wish would be granted.

For those of us who reside in *fault states,* such scenarios are certainly in the realm of possibility. That is why it makes sense to be apprised of the applicable fault grounds.

Fault Grounds for Divorce

In New York, as in most *fault states,* there are four fault grounds on which you can obtain a divorce. Some of these are pretty much self-explanatory. Starting with the most self-evident, the fault grounds are as follows:

Incarceration. Confinement of the defendant in prison for a period of three or more consecutive years after the marriage of the *plaintiff* (the moving spouse suing for divorce) and the *defendant* (the spouse being sued for divorce).

Adultery. This refers to the commission of a voluntary act of sexual or deviant sexual intercourse by the defendant with a person other than the plaintiff. Deviant sexual intercourse includes, but is not limited to, anal intercourse, fellatio, cunnilingus, pedophilia, zoophilia, and necrophilia.

Abandonment. This refers to desertion of the plaintiff by the defendant for a period of one or more years. Abandonment usually is physical, whereby one spouse moves out of the marital home and literally deserts the family.

There is also *constructive abandonment* (also known as *constructive sexual abandonment*). This ground is often used when both parties want to divorce as quickly as possible. One spouse without opposition will serve a complaint stating that the other spouse has refused to have sexual relations for more than one year. We will talk more about constructive abandonment later in this chapter.

Cruel and Inhuman Treatment. Conduct toward the plaintiff by the defendant that so endangers the physical or mental well-being of the plaintiff to make it unsafe or improper for the plaintiff to cohabit with the defendant.

The grounds of cruel and inhuman treatment is one that has various interpretations and legal ramifications. I think it would be instructive to examine some of them.

The whole concept of cruel and inhuman treatment goes to

the heart of the very personal way different couples interact. What may be a joke for one married couple might constitute a serious breach for another. Let me give one rather far-out example that recently came to my attention.

Picture an Orthodox Jewish couple, who are diligently observant of all religious precepts, including dietary laws. Husband and wife are in the midst of a bitter fight. As the husband is finishing up his Sabbath dinner, his wife informs him that she has purposely used nonkosher products as part of her cooking recipes.

"I basted your chicken with lard," the wife says, with a sarcastic grin on her face. "Since eating pork is forbidden to people of our faith, you have sinned."

Now, if the wife of a nonreligious Jew said that to her husband, it would probably be considered a laughing matter—or, at worst, a joke made in poor taste. However, in the case at hand, counsel could probably use that incident as part of other incidents showing a pattern of cruel and inhuman treatment.

While this example illustrates the need to evaluate the specific circumstances involved in a given relationship, there are many instances of cruel and inhuman treatment that apply to a broad range of people.

First, there is the troublesome issue of physical abuse. In one case that I handled, my client informed me that her husband once punched her in the stomach in front of her office building on a busy midtown Manhattan street. To make matters even worse, several of her coworkers witnessed the incident. This produced such great injury and embarrassment on the part of my client that she stayed out of work for a week.

As horrendous as this incident sounds, a judge might not necessarily find this single incident sufficient grounds for divorce. One of the tests would be the length of time the couple was married. Therefore, if the occurrence I just descibed happened between a couple who had been married for three months, a judge might well rule that it did indeed constitute sufficient grounds for divorce. Since my client and her husband had been married for eighteen years, one such aberration probably would not suffice. Unfortunately, though, this was not an isolated event.

As my client continued to describe her deteriorating marriage, a clear pattern of cruel and inhuman treatment emerged. The couple argued constantly—which, in and of itself, is not a basis for divorce. In this case, however, the husband frequently resorted to physical abuse.

Two years previously, immediately before leaving their house to attend a holiday dinner with the wife's family, the couple became embroiled in a loud argument. Before it was over, the husband had ripped the telephone out of the wall and thrown it at my client. The phone hit her on her right kneecap and caused a bad cut, which later became infected.

There were many other incidents of physical abuse over the years that my client could specifically recall. Since a number of these could be verified by reliable witnesses, the husband's attorney wisely counseled him to settle the matter out of court. The allegations of cruel and inhuman treatment could readily be established and would almost certainly be upheld by a judge.

As we observed in the case of the Orthodox Jewish couple, not all instances of cruel and inhuman treatment involve physical abuse. Let me give you a few more examples of the kinds of things that can constitute part of a pattern of cruel and inhuman treatment.

A wife was angry at her husband for staying out late playing cards with his male friends. In an attempt to get even, she called up her husband's employer and told him to watch her husband's actions carefully because he was on the verge of a nervous breakdown.

A husband and wife were driving home from a dinner party some thirty miles from their home. Two of their closest friends were in the back seat. The wife was chewing gum—a habit that greatly annoyed her husband. An argument ensued, and the husband threatened to force her out of the car unless she stopped chewing gum. Embarrassed and frightened that her husband was angry enough to follow through with his threat, the wife meekly discarded her gum.

Remember, there has to be a pattern of repeated cruel and inhuman treatment to qualify as a ground for divorce. In general, a single incident will not suffice. As the length of a marriage increases, the amount of cruel and inhuman treatment has to be

greater. The courts have held that what is enough to tear the
bonds of a short marriage is not enough to tear the bonds of a
longer marriage.

Another issue that the court considers in determining the
sufficiency of the proof is the severity of the incidents. I recall
one case in which the wife of a paraplegic husband kept hiding
his crutches so that he could not get around. On some bizarre
level, this could be interpreted as prankish and funny. In fact, it
is a rather extreme instance of cruel and inhuman treatment.

As a general rule, the most common examples of cruel and
inhuman treatment are somewhat less extreme. Nevertheless,
many involve physical assaults or intense verbal abuse in front of
family and friends. In any case, you can begin to see the potential for establishing fault on this basis.

We will get back to the practical value of allegations involving
cruel and inhuman treatment in obtaining a divorce. But first,
I'd like to cover the two nonfault grounds on which couples in
states like New York can file for divorce.

A Judgment of Separation (also called a **separation decree**).
This is based on the same four grounds of fault divorce described previously. In addition, lack of *child support* may be considered grounds for a separation decree, though not for a divorce. Finally, *abandonment* may be considered sufficient grounds
for separation, even if it is for less than one year.

Assuming that the husband and wife have lived separate and
apart for at least one year after the court issues a judgment of
separation, either spouse may then sue for a no-fault divorce.

Separation Agreement. When a husband and wife mutually
agree to divorce, and both desire to do so without allegations of
fault, they can sign a detailed contract that sets forth their respective rights and obligations in terms of distribution of property, maintenance, child support, custody, visitation, and all
other legal matters that pertain to the marriage.

Since this agreement will eventually be converted into a divorce, it must be drawn up in accordance with certain legal formalities. Therefore, you and your spouse will each require the

services of experienced marital attorneys to make sure there has been full financial disclosure, that the terms of the agreement are fair and equitable, and that all technical requirements have been met.

After a husband and wife have lived separate and apart, pursuant to a written agreement of separation for more than one year, either one may sue the other for a no-fault divorce. The only legal requirements are that the agreement was properly executed and that the plaintiff has lived up to its terms. At that point, the separation agreement is, in effect, legally converted into a divorce, which is also called a *conversion divorce*.

There are some practical drawbacks to having a separation agreement simply sit for a year. Let me tell you why I often advise clients to try to obtain a divorce immediately after executing a separation agreement.

By the time the parties agree—on dividing up their assets, on custody of children, and on everything else that goes into a separation agreement—they have essentially agreed to terminate the marriage. From an emotional standpoint, the parties no longer consider themselves married. And from a financial point of view, there are some definite risks in waiting a year to legally terminate the marriage.

One of the legal requirements of a separation agreement is that its terms were fair and reasonable at the time of the making of the agreement and are not unconscionable at the time of entry of final judgment. Let's see just how much significance these few words hold.

Frank and Joyce enter into a separation agreement. When the assets are divided, Frank receives stocks that were marital property and are valued at two hundred fifty thousand dollars. During the waiting period, Frank's stock escalates in value to one million dollars.

Exactly one year later, Frank tries to convert the separation agreement into a divorce. Not unexpectedly, Joyce decides to defend against the *conversion divorce*, claiming that the agreement is now unconscionable.

Because of this enormous financial change, this couple may now look at another period of litigation instead of a solution to

a failed marriage. In effect, they and their attorneys may have
to go back to square one in terms of resolving the financial aspects of the divorce.

   If you want to avoid the risk of doubling your emotional anguish—not to speak of your legal fees—I strongly advise you to
see if you can obtain a divorce immediately after the separation
agreement is signed.

   Okay, you are probably wondering how you can get around
the mandatory one-year waiting period necessary to convert a
separation agreement. The solution lies in then using the fault
grounds of the statute, particularly *constructive abandonment* or
cruel and inhuman treatment. If you or your spouse can honestly
demonstrate that your partner has refused to have sexual relations for more than one year without justification, or has engaged in a pattern of cruel and inhuman treatment, a divorce
may be granted on that basis.

   Most couples who take this route find it a relatively painless
solution. By the time estranged spouses have executed a separation agreement, such fault allegations are not likely to be particularly offensive to them. If the parties are required to appear,
the entire proceeding takes five or ten minutes at most. At times,
the divorce can be completed on papers alone without either
party having to appear in court. At that point, the matter is resolved and the parties can go on with their lives.

   We come now to the delicate situation of a married couple
living in a *fault state* when one party wants a divorce and the
other does not. Let's say, for example, that you are a wife who is
having an affair. You eventually admit this to your spouse and
announce your desire to divorce. Unfortunately, your husband
does not want to see the marriage end.

   In a *fault state* like New York, assuming he had proof other
than the wife's admissions, he could sue for divorce on the
grounds of *adultery.* The question is, however, what grounds do
you have—beyond a burning desire to end the marriage? The
answer often lies in the area of *cruel and inhuman treatment.*

   Before we go any further, let me state that no ethical attorney
is going to suggest or create a series of grounds that don't exist.
Your lawyer is not going to *suborn perjury.* Nevertheless, it is perfectly appropriate for an attorney to explain the grounds for di-

vorce to a client. In this context, counsel can legitimately explain or depict patterns of physical or mental cruelty that constitute *cruel and inhuman treatment.*

In many cases in which one of the spouses wishes to leave the marriage, there are interactions—often forgotten or intentionally buried—that have taken place between husband and wife that meet the test for cruel and inhuman treatment.

In an interview with a client, an attorney might ask the client if she and her spouse have engaged in a series of verbal or physical arguments in the course of the marriage. If the client answers that there have been no arguments or other proscribed conduct whatsoever, the issue is closed.

If, however, the client states that there has been a pattern of arguments, or physical violence, for example, the lawyer will proceed to ask the following kinds of questions:

- What was the nature of the arguments or physical violence?
- When did the arguments or physical violence take place?
- How frequently did they occur?
- Were there any witnesses to these incidents?
- Were the incidents provoked?

We, as human beings, tend to be forgetful, and to put unpleasant occurrences out of our minds. Frequently, however, once we start recalling a certain pattern of events, a floodgate of memory opens up. It is an attorney's job to help a client remember anything that might be of benefit to their obtaining the divorce. In a sense, the process is similar to a doctor exploring symptoms in trying to diagnose an illness.

When a physician interviews a patient, he or she often probes for information to determine an appropriate treatment program. Thus a doctor, in talking to a patient does not suggest that the person has pain. Rather, he asks the patient a series of questions designed to elicit the information necessary to make a correct diagnosis:

- Have you had pain?

- If so, where is the pain?
- Is the pain on the left or the right side?
- Is it a sharp or a dull pain?

In law, as in medicine, it is very difficult to make a meaningful diagnosis without engaging in a similar kind of probing. If it turns out that there is a pattern of cruel and inhuman treatment, an attorney might advise a client that there exist grounds to seek a divorce—even though this was an option that may not have initially occurred to the party.

As you might expect, there are some spouses living in *fault states* who have no legitimate grounds, save the wish to end the marriage. As an alternative, other than moving to another state, you may still over a period of time eventually be able to convince your spouse to listen to reason about obtaining a divorce.

If your spouse continues to hold onto the marriage despite your wishes, you might consider asking him or her to seek some appropriate individual or joint counseling. This may help him or her feel more like a collaborator in the decision and less like a victim. Hopefully, at that point, he or she will recognize the benefit of ending the marriage—and the ultimate wisdom of moving on to better things. If all else fails, you may just have to grimace and bear it.

Problems with a No-fault System

If you happen to live in a no-fault state, you do not have to worry about a spouse attempting to undermine your efforts to obtain a divorce. Still, despite its obvious advantages, the *no-fault divorce* system has more than its share of critics—and for good reason.

The no-fault laws were created to make divorce a less adversarial and traumatic experience. At the same time, such economic concepts as *community property, equitable distribution,* and *rehabilitative maintenance* were designed to tilt the scales of justice more in favor of women. Unfortunately, it hasn't quite turned out that way.

The laws, however well intentioned, have proved inequitable to women—particularly to nonworking mothers. As I mentioned previously, many of the new divorce statutes were instituted to reflect the changing social climate. In recent years, women have advocated their equal rights in virtually every social and economic area. And, while there has been some significant movement made in this direction, it is a fiction for the courts to act as though women have achieved anything close to equality.

Despite all the recent advances, women still overall have fewer job opportunities and less earning power than their male counterparts. This is particularly true of women of long-term marriages who have *physical custody* of their dependent children.

Studies indicate that in the wake of divorce estranged mothers are often forced to leave their middle-class homes for lives of abject poverty. On the other hand, their working, noncustodial husbands actually experience a significant improvement in their life-styles.

This unfortunate disparity has caused some knowledgeable observers to conclude that women fared better under the older and supposedly less equitable system. For one thing, the previous set of laws provided for permanent rather than temporary maintenance. This was based on the presumption that women were unable to compete with men in the workplace. By passing laws that acknowledge a wife's potential to forge her own career, the state legislatures have failed to recognize the existing gap between future potential and present reality.

Aside from these oversights and inequities, I still believe that the lawmakers of most states are making a sincere effort to reflect the social and economic upheaval our society has undergone in the past few decades. In any case, we have come too far to turn back the clock. For better or worse, *no-fault divorce* is a fact of life in an ever-increasing number of states.

It is important to recognize that we are still in the midst of a prolonged transition period in terms of male–female relationships. Furthermore, any difficulties that might exist between a husband and wife under normal circumstances are immeasurably exacerbated by the divorce process. It is unrealistic to expect the courts to provide recompense to the aggrieved spouse for the kinds of intimate and personal issues divorce brings to the fore.

In view of all this, I can only reiterate some key points that apply whether you live in a fault or a no-fault state:

SEVEN PRECEPTS FOR WINNING AT DIVORCE

- Learn everything you can about the financial, legal, and emotional aspects of divorce.
- Find yourself a good attorney who will help steer you through this complex process.
- If necessary, seek out marital or divorce counseling.
- Work closely with the professionals on your team to establish and pursue realistic and equitable financial and child-care goals.
- Try to make decisions that you will feel good about down the road.
- Do everything reasonable you can to stay out of court.
- Don't ever forget that your destiny is in your hands.

9

The Legal Process of
Ending a Marriage

Fɪʀsᴛ, let me mention some good news. There is a strong
probability that most of you will not have to go through the
anguish and the expense of a divorce trial. Nevertheless, you can
expect your attorney to move forward as though you were
headed in that direction, even while he or she is actively engaged
in attempting to negotiate a favorable settlement.

In taking this two-track approach to your case, your attorney
will be gathering the legal and factual materials that form the
basis of a successful trial. At the same time, he or she will be
using those facts and legal precedents to strengthen your negotiating position. A competent, ethical lawyer will always be working toward a settlement, while making it clear that you are willing
to go to trial if it becomes necessary.

Whether or not your case is ultimately contested in front of
a judge, counsel will want to obtain as much information from
you and your spouse as possible. He or she will accomplish this
by gathering the relevant facts of your case through discussions
with you and examination of any records you can provide. After
the data have been cataloged and categorized, your attorney can
conduct discovery to obtain information from your spouse, then
he or she can begin the process of negotiating on your behalf.
Optimally, a satisfactory settlement will be reached at some point
in negotiations. If not, you and your spouse will wind up fighting
it out in court.

Although it is not important for you to be fluent in the tech-
nicalities of proceeding with a lawsuit in a matrimonial action, I

would like you to be apprised of some of the basics so that you will understand how your attorney is proceeding on your behalf. Although the legal terms and procedures will vary from state to state, I will use New York as a generally representative example of how a case proceeds.

The Summons

A divorce action is commenced by service of a summons by the *plaintiff* (the moving party) upon the *defendant* (the person who is being sued). A summons contains the names and addresses of the parties, the name of the court in which the plaintiff is suing, and the county in which the action is commenced (also called the venue). A divorce action can commence in the county where the plaintiff or the defendant resides. As a rule, venue is not an important issue in divorce suits.

The summons is addressed to the defendant, stating that he or she is required to serve a *notice of appearance* within twenty days. A summons must also state the grounds upon which the divorce is sought, as well as providing a brief statement of the kind of *relief* that is being sought in a final judgment.

The first *relief* a plaintiff would seek is the divorce itself. The second relief might be a declaration of *separate property*—as opposed to *marital property*. You may also ask for custody of the children or for legal fees during the course of the action (or *pendente lite*). All such requests would be outlined in a series of very brief, single-line statements in the appropriate place on the summons.

Complaint and Counterclaim

The *complaint* is the second legal document that is served in a divorce suit. It is also the first of the *pleadings*. The complaint sets forth, in some detail, the basis and framework of the action. While it need not be enormously detailed, the *complaint* does have to contain enough particulars to apprise the defendant of the nature and specific details of the suit.

The defendant has twenty days after service of the complaint to serve his or her answer. This, then, is the third legal step in a divorce case. In answering the complaint, a defendant may admit or deny specific portions contained in that document. He or she may also issue a *counterclaim,* which is simply a responsive complaint on the part of the defendant.

Simply put, when the plaintiff files his or her charges, that is called a complaint. When the defendant responds by filing his or her charges, it is called a *counterclaim.* Essentially, both documents contain the same kinds of information and allegations.

Now, in some cases, the defendant may be opposed to the divorce. If so, the attorney can go into court and file a motion to dismiss the complaint on the basis of a procedural problem, such as insufficient grounds, a jurisdictional infraction—or a number of other legal issues. If any of these are upheld, the plaintiff is basically back to square one in terms of pursuing a divorce action. Assuming, however, that the parties and their attorneys can satisfy the requirements of the *pleading* stage, they will then be ready for the next major phase of the case.

Discovery

As I mentioned previously, one of the first steps your attorney will take when the two of you start working together is to attempt to learn as much as possible about the facts of your case. Initially, he or she will accomplish this by talking to you and reviewing any written documentation that you are able to produce. Ultimately, however, this is only part of the picture. In order to determine the true strength of your case, your attorney will need to find out as much as possible about your spouse. This is the crux of the *discovery* process.

Depending on the circumstances, discovery can also be obtained on such issues as custody, fault, and grounds. In most cases, however, the emphasis is on matters of finance. Therefore, the process frequently begins with the attorneys exchanging relevant financial documents and records.

Generally, the first formal step in discovery is to serve a *net-worth statement.* This tends to be a rather lengthy and involved document, spelling out all sorts of financial information pertaining to the marriage.

In addition to providing comprehensive financial statements, the two attorneys may have a series of telephone conferences during which additional financial information will be requested. Counsel may, for example, ask the other attorney to provide copies of his client's tax returns for the past five years. Such documents are exchanged as a matter of course. In fact, if you sense that the lawyers are engaged in some kind of adversarial battle or ego trip at this early stage in the proceedings, you had better nip it in the bud—or else consider retaining new counsel.

As the *discovery* process moves forward, the attorneys may employ any or all of the following legal instruments.

Interrogatories. After your attorney receives the financial statement from your spouse's counsel, he or she may present the other side with written questions—or *interrogatories*—for the purpose of obtaining additional information. Interrogatories are generally quite extensive, often fifteen to twenty pages. Let me give you a brief illustration of the function of written interrogatories.

Assume that a husband, in his statement of net worth, made reference to a particular bank account. An attorney might require further information, such as: When was the account opened? When was it closed? How long was the money in the bank? Were there any large withdrawals in the past three years? All these questions must be answered in writing and under oath.

Notices of discovery and inspection are requests for the other side to produce documents for your attorney's examination and copying. Such inspection takes place either at the courthouse or at the offices of one of the attorneys. Counsel may serve such notices after obtaining the *interrogatories,* or at the same time that these written questions are being served.

Basically, *notices of discovery and inspection* are just what the name implies. Your lawyer wants the other side to produce certain financial records—such as loan agreements, bank statements, income tax returns, pension information, salary information, credit card information, partnership agreements, monthly brokerage house statements—and any other appropriate forms of documentary data.

Once all this information has been gathered and the interrogatories have been served, the attorneys may proceed with the next discovery tool.

Oral Depositions. This refers to an attorney's oral questioning of the adverse party. Such questioning may take place at the courthouse or at the lawyer's office, in the presence of a *court reporter*. A deposition is also interchangeably referred to as an *examination before trial* (or an EBT).

You may, in certain circumstances, be able to inquire as to the fault allegations in the complaint. Generally speaking, however, an attorney cannot ask questions about the underlying grounds for the divorce.

If in fact your case proceeds to trial, the court has to make an accurate determination of marital assets and the relative circumstances of the spouses in order to make an appropriate division. Therefore, it places virtually no limits on the scope of relevant financial information that may be inquired about to determine marital assets.

Let's assume, for example, that documents indicate that a husband closed a particular bank account, which at the time had a ten-thousand-dollar balance. Under such circumstances, the wife's attorney might ask the following questions:

- What was the origin of that money?
- What did you use the money for after you withdrew it from the bank?
- How soon can you produce the records showing what you did with the money?
- Was there a conversation between you and your wife at the time the money was taken out of the bank?
- If so, what did each of you say to the other?
- Was there an agreement as to what was going to be done with the ten thousand dollars?

Appraisals

As your attorney proceeds with discovery, various appraisers may have to be retained to determine the present worth of a pension, the likely selling price of the marital home, or the value of a professional license or a business. In cases in which one of the spouses is involved in a cash business, there is often a reluctance to supply the information to the appraisers.

Under such circumstances, the husband's lawyer may refuse to voluntarily permit an investigation by the wife's accountant. In some instances, counsel may state a willingness to comply with a financial investigation, but then supply only a small portion of the information needed to make a meaningful appraisal. Counsel may take the position that sufficient information is not available, or that, since his client owns only 50 percent of the company's stock, he can't obtain permission from the other stockholders to disclose this information.

At that point, the wife's attorney would have to go into court and make a *motion* to obtain the necessary information. As I said earlier, virtually anything that sheds light on the assets of the parties is discoverable. Even if the husband is a minority stockholder in a closed corporation, the courts in most states will direct that this information about the corporation be made available—if it is required to make an accurate determination.

Nevertheless, judges sometimes find themselves faced with a situation in which issues of *discovery* are pitted against those of confidentiality. Let's take an example of a wife in a particularly bitter divorce battle who is trying to ascertain the value of her husband's law practice. In order to determine how much her husband's firm is worth, the wife demands a complete list of clients. Naturally, the wife is aware that if her attorney began calling up all of her husband's clients and started pressuring them for information about fees paid, this could prove most embarrassing.

While most judges would not permit the husband to stonewall, neither would they allow the wife to use the *discovery* process as a way to vent her bitterness. In a circumstance of this sort, the court would generally try to fashion a remedy that permits the discovery without revealing the names of the husband's clients.

For example, a judge might find that the husband's law firm had recently submitted financial statements to a bank in connection with a loan. Common sense would dictate that such a statement is likely to be reasonably accurate. If anything, there is a tendency to overstate the value of assets when applying for a loan. The judge, therefore, might balance the issue of entitlement to *discovery* with the question of confidentiality by allowing discovery of the loan application but not of the firm's client list.

When you are attempting to determine the value of a cash business, you must be prepared to assist your attorney in tracking down elusive documentation. One technique that is helpful during this aspect of discovery is maintaining the kind of financial diary we discussed in chapter 3.

Now, let's assume you've completed the financial aspect of the case. That's one hydra head. If there are children, questions of *child custody* and *visitation* may also be issues for *discovery*. If so, the procedures are much the same as those used in the financial areas.

Psychological Evaluations

You may, for example, have written *interrogatories* and oral *depositions* pertaining to the relative fitness of each parent to maintain *child custody*. Instead of the accountants and appraisers associated with financial discovery, your attorney may rely on the testimony of psychiatrists, psychologists, or social workers to support your position. Such testimony would be directed toward the various standards that the court may look at in determining custody and visitation. Toward that end, the parties and the children may be requested to submit to examination by a mental health professional.

As the case proceeds, a variety of problems and disputes can come up. If so, an attorney can prepare specific *motions*, petitioning the court to grant one or more *temporary orders* of *relief*. I'll briefly discuss the most common kinds of relief that are requested during such *motion practice*.

When a couple is engaged in a bitter custody dispute, there are often threats of emotional and physical coercion. In order to spare the children, a judge will often award temporary *child custody* to one parent, while specifically defining the other's *visitation* rights.

If there is a pattern of physical or emotional violence in the relationship, one or both of the spouses may have their attorneys petition the court for an *order of exclusive occupancy*. This would grant one of the spouses (generally the one maintaining custody of the children) sole temporary rights to live in the marital home.

If it can be shown that one of the parties is physically abusing the other spouse and/or the children, the other spouse can seek an *order of protection*. This document specifically orders the abusive spouse to cease these destructive behaviors. That spouse may also be instructed to stay away from the family member(s) who have allegedly been abused. A violation of such an order can lead to arrest.

There are also some *motions* that pertain to financial areas. If, for example, a wife fears that her husband may attempt to hide or dissipate assets, she may ask her attorney to seek a *temporary restraining order* or preliminary injunction. This would prevent the husband from spending, hiding, or transferring, without a court order, any assets that may be construed as marital property.

In a large percentage of divorce cases, there is disagreement between the spouses over how much the monied spouse should pay in terms of temporary *maintenance* and temporary *child support*. When that happens, the custodial parent's attorney will request these forms of temporary relief while the action is pending (i.e., *pendente lite*) along with preliminary *motions* for *child custody*, for *visitation*, and for *exclusive occupancy* of the marital residence.

There is often a lot of "Sturm und Drang" taking place as these financially based motions are being filed—with accusations being tossed back and forth between the parties. At this point, however, the court has no interest in who is at fault and why. The court's only concern with such *pendente lite* motions are the temporary needs of the nonmonied spouse and the children during the course of the litigation.

If the nonmonied spouse does not have sufficient funds to pay her attorney, the court may order that *interim counsel fees* be paid by the monied spouse. Furthermore, if the nonmonied spouse cannot afford the costs involved in the discovery process, the court may order *expert witness fees* to pay for appraisers, accountants, and other experts whose testimony may be necessary.

Trial vs. Settlement

Once all the necessary financial and other information has been obtained and all the appropriate motions have been decided, the parties and their attorneys find themselves at a critical juncture in the case. I find that most couples reach a settlement during the course of *discovery*. In those cases that are not resolved, the attorney will prepare the appropriate papers in order to obtain a court date for a trial. In New York, such legal papers are called a *note of issue* and a *notice of trial*.

Again, keep in mind that the vast majority of divorce cases are never actually contested in court. Therefore, all the time your attorney is proceeding toward a trial, he or she is doing so with the knowledge that a settlement will probably be negotiated. If the parties and their lawyers are at all rational, most cases should be settled at some appropriate time during the discovery process.

By the time the attorneys have completed their discovery process and depositions and filed all their motions, most couples have worn themselves out in terms of legal proceedings, monetary costs, and emotional anxiety. At that point, nobody is in much of a mood to fight anymore. Husband and wife have both had ample opportunity to vent their anger, and even the more litigious lawyers should have sated their adversarial instincts. Generally speaking, the time is now right for a more rational climate to prevail.

Immediately after discovery has been completed, a *note of issue* may be filed. In some cases, however, the parties are on the verge of settling, so this step is really pro forma. Nevertheless, until the settlement is finalized, counsel may well continue moving simultaneously on the track that leads toward a trial.

I find it unfortunate that most people go into a divorce action with no real concept of what the process entails. One of this book's functions is to arm you with a practical understanding of the financial, legal, and emotional issues you may have to face. I hope that the increased knowledge and awareness you obtain from these chapters will help you assume a more positive and rational approach.

I've seen too many estranged husbands and wives attempt to use the legal system as a means of achieving emotional recompense. This is especially true of the spouse who perceives himself or herself as the injured party. What such a person is usually looking for is revenge—either legally or financially. Most of the time, he or she is unable to get either one.

A reasonable attorney faced with such a client often finds himself between a rock and a hard place. Counsel may see a clear and appropriate solution to dividing the marital assets and solving the custody and visitation issues. He or she may recognize this as a good deal for the client and one that the other side would consider in the right ballpark. If, however, a client wants to engage in economic blackmail and other hardball tactics, he or she doesn't want to hear about sensible solutions, and the attorney who tries to force this view on such a client may soon be replaced by another lawyer.

Every divorce negotiation has a life of its own. Therefore, nothing can ever be resolved until the parties reach a settlement capability. Attorneys in this field come to understand that until both spouses are ready to settle, it's just not going to happen. You can tear yourself apart on a case, but you're only aggravating yourself for nothing.

Often, people have to go through a catharsis before they are ready to settle. They may have to talk to every one of their friends and do all sorts of things to purge themselves of their hate and anxiety. Fortunately, most rational men and women eventually reach a point at which they can accept reality. Only then will they say to counsel: "Please help me put this situation to rest so I can get on with my life."

The Pretrial Conference

If, after all this, the parties are still unable to settle, they and their counsel will have to undergo this next legal step. Actually, the pretrial conference often consists of a series of conferences during which a judge attempts to help the parties resolve their differences so that a full-blown trial will not become necessary. In some instances, the *conference judge* is not the same one who will actually be trying the case. In New York, the trial judge's law secretary (who is also an attorney) frequently presides over pretrial conferences.

While the guidance offered by the *conference judge* is not legally binding, significant pressure to resolve the outstanding issues can be brought to bear. If, for example, the pretrial judge senses that both attorneys have agreed on a reasonable settlement that is being held up by warring spouses, he may try to help the attorneys to get the parties to settle. Let's look at how this might transpire in a case in which the amount of the distributive award could not be resolved.

First, the *conference judge* or the law secretary would hold a private conference with the husband's attorney. In the course of the conference, the judge might take counsel into chambers and, perhaps, say something of the following sort:

"I have never encountered a situation in which a husband has gotten away with as much as your client. But for some reason, the wife is willing to take it. The wife's attorney is offering you a great deal. If I were in your position, I would settle—because if the case goes to trial, I have a feeling that you are going to get stuck for a lot more money."

Shortly thereafter, the same judge would then hold a private conference in chambers with the wife's attorney. There, he or she would employ the same kind of psychology, advising counsel as follows:

"In my opinion, the wife is asking for far too much. If I were the judge trying this case, there is absolutely no way you could wind up with anything close to what you're asking for. You would be well-advised to rethink your position."

At that point, the *conference judge* might ask both parties to go out with their attorneys for lunch—asking them to come back in the afternoon and confer with him again. Only, this time, he would expect them to demonstrate a better understanding of life's realities.

In addition to the urgings of the conference judge, there are additional pressures on the parties to settle. For one thing, there is often a wait of six months to a year between the time a *note of issue* is filed and when the case actually goes to trial. Only the most hard-bitten warriors are ready to continue putting their lives on hold in order to fight it out in court.

In general, the small percentage of cases that go beyond the pretrial conference stage involve one of four basic scenarios:

- One or both clients—or their attorneys—are completely unreasonable or irrational.

- Both sides may be reasonable. However, there is an intractable difference in interpreting the law as it relates to one or more critical issues in the case.

- There is an honest disagreement in the valuation of a major asset or about the income of a spouse.

- There is an honest disagreement over the issue of custody or visitation and what is in the child's best interest.

I would not suggest that you forgo your legal rights, harm your child, or impoverish yourself just to avoid going to trial. That would be highly irrational. The decision to settle or go to trial, however, must be based on a number of factors: What is the cost—in terms of time, money and emotions? What are the likely results of each course of action? What will the short- and long-term impact be on you and your children?

If you find yourself unable to be rational, seek counseling and urge your spouse to do the same. If the attorneys are hung up on some point of legal contention, press them to find a reasonable middle ground. Perhaps you or your spouse can give in on that one sticking point in exchange for a more favorable settlement on another issue.

Remember, one of the keys to winning at this game is to retain as much control as possible. As long as the negotiating process continues, you can play a major role in shaping the ultimate solution. Once your case goes to trial, however, you have conceded that you and your spouse are incapable of resolving your own differences.

The moment negotiations cease and the outcome is placed in the hands of a third party (however handsomely titled and robed), you have essentially given up your right to determine your own future. Under the circumstances, I can only say to you what I say to friends who are about to spend a weekend in Las Vegas or Atlantic City: "Good luck when you roll the dice!"

10

Leaving Home

N ow that we've looked at some of the legal, financial, and emotional ramifications of divorce, let's further explore how this whole package of complex and often contradictory variables can conspire to turn the process of breaking up from a comparatively normal part of the human condition into a veritable nightmare.

You've probably heard the expression, "Home is where the heart is." I've always found this an apt, if somewhat romantic, way to envision a loving, cohesive family unit. When a marriage begins to dissolve, however, the same home that was once a thriving family's material and spiritual center can, with terrible quickness, become transformed into a hostile war zone.

Many divorces are preceded by a physical separation in which one of the spouses wishes to abandon the family dwelling. But while the heart may feel an overpowering desire to leave, legal doctrine may compel the body to remain.

Conflict and turmoil run high when a marriage begins to disintegrate. The emotional health of parents and children can deteriorate if embattled spouses remain under the same roof. Indeed, the well-being of all family members may be best served if one spouse does leave. In many instances, however, legal reality virtually forecloses what would otherwise be a sensible solution, particularly in fault states like New York.

The spouse who voluntarily moves out may suffer serious damage to his or her legal position in an impending divorce. The simple act of staying, however, can result in a continuous and disabling conflict for both spouses as well as for the children. In effect, an open wound is left to fester. Meanwhile, a cumbersome legal process slowly wends its way toward a solution—one that, with each passing day, becomes less likely to yield satisfactory results for any of the adults or children involved.

We have not, as yet, fully discussed the issues of *child custody* and protecting the interests of children—who are, after all, the most tragic and helpless victims of divorce. Nevertheless, I have already cited numerous examples of how much more dramatic the entire divorce process becomes when children are involved. The reasons for this are about to become even more apparent.

It is my strong belief that divorcing spouses, as well as the professionals who serve them, have a special obligation to do what they can to alleviate this devastation. Unfortunately, these ethical responsibilities are often obliterated by the conflicting needs and goals of the spouses, their attorneys, and therapists. This complex package is further exacerbated by a legal system that often approaches the "leaving home" problem in a manner deficient and insensitive to the needs of divorcing spouses and their children.

I think it would be useful to explore this issue from the points of view of all involved: an entire family—as well as their attorneys and therapists—and to examine how this unsavory mix is aided by an unresponsive legal system. I will also offer a number of suggestions for substantial changes in the policies, not only of the courts, but of the attorneys and mental health professionals as well.

It is my hope that this integrated approach will help separating and near-separating spouses become more aware of the pitfalls they may encounter. I believe that it will also provide a valuable object lesson for anyone who is either experiencing, or interested in, the dynamics of marriage and divorce.

In the end, the package of variables that enters into the leaving-home scenario is a microcosm of the inherent problems of the entire divorce process—particularly in a *fault state*. Each spouse has his or her own particular set of needs and goals. The same is true for the respective attorneys and mental health professionals. Lastly, there are the needs of the children—whose vulnerability and ultimate interests should take precedence above all others.

In this chapter and elsewhere, I refer to an interdisciplinary approach to divorce. In essence, this is a call to legal and mental health professionals to work together at focusing on the long-term interests of the clients and their families. Although I take pride in being one who is at the forefront of attempting to develop a productive dialogue between the two professions, I am painfully aware of how far we have to go before true cooperation becomes the rule rather than the exception.

In the meantime, I must come back to the concept that people hold the key to their own destinies. Let me take that a step further. The outcome of your marriage, separation, or divorce is in your hands. Professionals can help you, but don't expect them to take control. As far as the legal system is concerned, pray that you never reach a point at which you must depend on a trial to resolve your problems and delve out justice. For it is only then that you will be fully aware of the dire consequences of passing your fate into the hands of others.

That said, I invite you to explore the plight of a typical family pulled apart by the leaving-home scenario. We will look at this multidimensional landscape from the point of view of a husband and wife, their two children, two New York City attorneys, and three therapists. But let me first introduce you to the members of the Gold family:

Family Members:	
Irv Gold	age 36
Sue Gold	age 35
David Gold	age 9 1/2
Roberta Gold	age 7

A Family History

Irv, the second of four children of a middle-class couple, grew up with a strong sense of right and wrong. He was a Merit Scholarship finalist and an Eagle Scout. Irv has been married twice. His first marriage was to the daughter of a close family friend.

Just before the wedding, Irv had serious misgivings but refused to call off the ceremony because he did not want to hurt his fiancée, who was someone he had known all his life.

While Irv has many acquaintances he refers to as friends, he does not feel particularly close to any of them. He keeps personal problems to himself and tends to withdraw if someone angers him. Irv sees any display of negative feelings as a failure on his part.

After eighteen months, Irv divorced his first wife. Four years later, he met Sue, his present spouse.

Sue Gold is the youngest of three children and has two older brothers. Her mother was a housewife, who never had outside employment. Her father, a heavy drinker, worked as a traveling salesman.

Sue graduated from a commercial high school, where she took a secretarial curriculum. She did not have many close friends and preferred to stay at home with her mother.

Irv and Sue met through mutual friends and married in a civil ceremony after a six-month courtship.

Both describe the first few years of marriage as being financially difficult. Shortly after the wedding, Irv began an M.B.A. program but was forced to drop out when his father became seriously ill. After Irv's father died, he took over the family business, a neighborhood haberdashery store.

In declaring his love, Irv vowed that he would take care of Sue, whom he saw as fragile and vulnerable. He helped with chores around the house and spent time shopping with her. Considering that Irv worked long hours, he took a very active role in planning meals and organizing the home. Sue came to rely on Irv's participation in these matters.

Irv felt flattered and proud to be so needed by his wife. As time went on, he became more and more intense about his relationship with Sue, neglecting friendships and outside interests.

Sue enjoyed her life with Irv. He was attentive, kind, and dependable. The couple planned to have children in the near future. Although she worried about how pregnancy might affect her looks and the condition of her body, Sue felt certain Irv would be accepting and supportive.

During this period, the couple was getting along well. Sue encouraged Irv to become involved in various business endeavors, always expressing confidence in his ability. Although she wished her daily life to be more active, Sue could not find the energy to pursue new and challenging endeavors.

After Irv's business improved, he sold the store and went into insurance/investments as an independent agent. Irv was successful at this new venture, and within two years he was earning an annual income in excess of $100,000.

The family moved from an apartment to a four-bedroom house in an upscale suburb. About a year later, their first child, David, was born. Sue stayed home and cared for the baby. Because of his flexible work hours, Irv was able to keep his business prospering while still looking after his wife and their infant son.

Two years later, Roberta was born. Irv became even more involved in child care and planned to minimize being away from home. Shortly thereafter, the family purchased a year-round vacation home about an hour away.

As time went by, Irv started feeling stuck in a rut professionally and decided to complete his M.B.A. Sue, who had become increasingly dependent on her husband's contributions around the house, expressed fears that school would take Irv away from the family.

Irv completed his degree in two and a half years. At about the same time, he became romantically involved with the mother of one of his son's classmates, whom he had met through the P.T.A. His lover was a successful civil engineer, previously divorced from a childless marriage that had lasted two years.

Irv and his lover carried on their secret affair for eight months. At that point, Sue learned of her husband's infidelity through an anonymous phone call. Somehow, she knew it was true, though she didn't necessarily feel that it signaled the end of the marriage. But Irv had different ideas. After eleven years together, Irv told Sue that he wanted a divorce.

At first, Sue was shocked, hurt, and disbelieving. Nevertheless, she was still hopeful that Irv would change his mind. Irv, for his part, felt increasingly guilty about Sue's sadness. He was also very concerned about how a divorce might affect the two children. Irv decided to seek professional counseling and encouraged Sue to do the same. But in spite of the counseling of competent mental health professionals, the emotional situation continued to deteriorate.

Early in Irv's therapy, the following pattern of behavior emerged: Irv would angrily insist upon a divorce, then would retreat in guilt when Sue expressed sadness or undying love for him. In his confusion, Irv would revert to his familiar helper role. Inevitably, these ambivalent feelings only increased his frustration and anger—leading to more bitter and frequent confrontations. The children were beginning to show signs of distress, thus adding to his guilt.

Sue eventually became convinced that Irv would not change his mind about ending the marriage. This caused her to take a hardened stance. She became more adamant that she would never consent to a divorce and that Irv would have no access to the children if he left.

Irv and Sue both consulted attorneys. Initially, Irv proposed a separation with generous terms for both the division of assets and maintenance—if Sue would agree to joint physical custody of the children. Sue, however, insisted that the children belonged at home with her and refused to consider any other arrangement.

As time passed, Sue became more openly hostile to Irv, more uncooperative and unpredictable. She often provoked confrontations, though Irv tried his best to avoid face-to-face hostility. To allay her growing feelings of depression, Sue began to confide in neighbors, teachers at the children's school, and local shopkeepers. She had never before been so open about her problems, but now she was evoking a great deal of much-needed sympathy.

By this time, the children had become visibly upset. David would side with whichever parent spoke to him first, while Roberta withdrew and became more distant. Irv insisted upon consulting a child psychiatrist, who suggested therapy for the children. She also stressed how essential it was that the parents resolve their differences as soon as possible.

If they wanted to preserve their children's emotional health, the psychiatrist informed them, Sue and Irv would either have to stay together or get divorced. One way or the other, they could not continue to live under the same roof and allow David and Roberta to bear witness to such destructive behavior.

Unfortunately, the child psychiatrist's advice was largely ignored, as the arguments between husband and wife continued to escalate. Irv became more openly angry and verbally threatening. Both Irv and Sue sought to prove how uncaring or how poor a parent the other was. Irv compared Sue to other women, while Sue provoked frequent arguments. And, despite the child psychiatrist's admonitions, these confrontations often took place in front of David and Roberta.

On one occasion, Sue had the door locks changed, and Irv smashed a patio window to gain access. On another occasion, Sue threw a bowl of salad against the kitchen wall, claiming that Irv had prepared the salad to prove to the children that he was the better parent. As Sue became more hostile, Irv became concerned for his physical safety. Sue had actually hinted that Irv might be in danger as he slept.

Upon the advice of his attorney, Irv had a lock put on the door to the guest bedroom—where he had been staying for over six months. In order to decrease contact with Sue, he would spend evenings either out with the children or all alone, locked in his room.

Irv's sleep deteriorated. He was showing signs of anxiety and clinical depression. Although he was able to do his work, his concentration was poor. Irv was also becoming increasingly upset with the children, especially if they became involved in the arguments. Once, after a particularly hostile confrontation with Sue, Irv absentmindedly drove through a red light, struck a car, and sustained minor injuries.

Sue had started calling the police during their arguments. She registered ten different complaints, but the officers were loath to become involved. On at least four occasions, Irv was awakened by the police answering emergency calls to the home, where he was allegedly beating Sue. On each occasion, they found no evidence of physical violence. They did, however, find an obviously disturbed Sue. Although the police were sympathetic to Irv, they suggested that he leave home to allay the situation.

Sue sought an *order of protection*. Irv, in turn, did the same. Sue delayed hearings on the orders, claiming that she was ill. The situation had reached crisis proportions for the spouses— and especially for the children. Together with their therapists and attorneys, the Golds are now attempting to work out a solution. Let's examine the situation, first from the point of view of the three therapists, then from the perspective of the two attorneys.

The Mental Health Perspective
THE HUSBAND'S THERAPIST

When Irv first came into treatment, his reasons were two-fold. The present marriage was his second, and, obviously heading for divorce, Irv felt compelled to examine his role in choosing unsuitable mates. The primary reason he gave for seeking therapy, however, was to gain knowledge about how to minimize the worsening trauma for the children.

Initially, Irv was reasonable and intent upon settling this dispute. He denied any anger toward Sue, stating only that the marriage was a mistake. He was, however, unconsciously hostile and provocative, which inflamed the arguments. As Irv began to express his anger more openly in therapy, these provocations lessened.

Irv's therapist is becoming increasingly concerned about Irv's depression and impulsive outbursts of anger. Irv has also started to demonstrate a severe sleep disturbance but refuses to take sleep medication—insisting that he hates taking pills of any kind. Irv has finally admitted that he is fearful and suspicious about Sue's hostility and what she might do if he allows himself to lapse into a deep sleep.

Irv is feeling isolated in his home. He also feels hurt and embittered by his neighbors' rejection of him and their seeming acceptance of Sue's complaints and lies.

Irv is starting to despair that the fights will never end, that divorce will never come, and that a normalization of relations with the children will never take place. This leaves Irv feeling hopeless and frustrated.

In cases like this, the therapist often prescribes antidepressant medication; however, she rejects this approach for Irv as a "quick fix." What concerns her far more is addressing the situational causes of Irv's problems.

Irv's attorney has insisted that he remain in this stressful household. Yet the therapist is concerned about further erosion to Irv's personality and capacity to function if he remains in the home. Irv's therapist encourages him to confront his attorney so as to force an alternative.

THE WIFE'S THERAPIST

Sue's therapist sees a victimized patient struggling to overcome her passivity and dependence upon a man who no longer loves her. He encourages Sue to assert herself, gain support of friends, and increase her self-esteem by assuming more responsibility for her life—and staking a claim to the marital home.

At the therapist's suggestion, Sue has started a modest business at home, selling a nationally distributed chain of health-and-beauty products. It will take some time for this to generate a substantial income, but it seems to be having a positive effect.

Sue is harmed by delay in resolving the marital dispute because it allows her to hope that Irv will change his mind. Sue's therapist has been convinced for some time that Irv will not do so.

The therapist is pressing Sue to ask her attorney to have Irv removed from the home before something violent happens. The therapist has suggested that Sue take the children to her parents if relations become too threatening. Sue reports, however, that her attorney does not support this action without actual proof that bodily harm has occurred. Sue's therapist is also concerned that the attorney may have subtly suggested that Sue provoke Irv to hit her in order to strengthen her case.

THE CHILDREN'S THERAPIST

The child psychologist met with both parents as part of her evaluation. She found that the children were both suffering, albeit in different ways.

The parental fighting has become an ever-increasing source of fear and sadness for the children. Irv has assured them that although he wishes to leave their mother, he has no intention of ever leaving them.

Sue, meanwhile, has explained to the children that their father plans to desert her *and* them. At times, each parent has asked the children to act as witnesses against the other.

David's response has been to agree with the parent with whom he has last spoken, often changing positions. Between his mother's tears and his father's demand for loyalty, David is feeling terribly confused.

The young boy has started to have nightmares. Before his parent's conflict, David's school performance was above average and he had important friendships. Now, for the first time, he has angry outbursts in school and at play, and he has lost at least two of his closest friends.

Roberta has become more quiet and reserved in the wake of the growing hostility between her mother and father. She refuses to take sides when asked by either parent and appears almost indifferent to their struggles. In school, she daydreams and does not participate in activities. When the teacher asks what's wrong, Roberta denies that there are problems. One obvious symptom that something is troubling her is that she has started to wet her bed after not doing so since the age of three.

The children need certainty about their futures. They are attached to both parents and are afraid because these relationships are deteriorating. Time is working against the children. As their symptoms worsen, their parents are becoming less able to deal with them.

The Attorneys' Perspectives
THE HUSBAND'S ATTORNEY

Irv's attorney has counseled him as follows: "The essential problem is that, if you voluntarily move out of the marital house, you will be unable to return. By doing so, you will also, in effect, agree that your wife should be the children's primary custodian.

"It is highly unlikely that you can obtain exclusive occupancy of the house by evicting your wife. To accomplish this, you will have to show physical or mental abuse or its probability. That would be the only way to establish that eviction is necessary to protect life or property. Though your wife is hostile and confrontational and has hinted of future physical violence, her conduct has not been serious enough to make a credible case that would compel a court to evict her.

"If you leave voluntarily, you will almost surely not be able to return. All that your wife need show to keep you out is that your return is likely to cause domestic strife. She should be able to do so, given that she does not want you back.

"Furthermore, if you leave voluntarily you will reduce to virtually zero your chances of obtaining custody of your children. The standard for determining custody is ostensibly the gender-neutral test of the best interests of the child.

"In reality, most courts still favor the mother as the custodial parent for young children, unless she is clearly unfit. Although you have been involved in your children's day-to-day care, your wife is still unquestionably David's and Roberta's primary caretaker.

"If you move out, you concede that your wife is a fit custodian for your children. Otherwise, you risk their health and safety by moving out. If you move out and leave your children in the care of an unfit parent, you call your own parental fitness into question.

"In addition, by moving out, you make a statement that the children are better off living with your wife. Courts try to maintain stability in a child's life. You face an uphill fight to convince a court that you should be the children's custodian after you leave. Courts generally give priority to the child's first custody arrangement, whether it is reached voluntarily or by court order after preliminary litigation. Therefore, it is very likely that a voluntary temporary arrangement will become permanent.

"While it may be in your emotional interests to move, doing so will seriously compromise your legal position. Stay put, de-

spite an anticipated long and unhappy conflict. Use your therapy to deal with the strain."

THE WIFE'S ATTORNEY

Sue's attorney has counseled her as follows: "You do not have a
serious chance of getting a court to order your husband out of
the house. The complaints of your husband's physical violence
are not corroborated by objective evidence. Your repeated and
unfounded calls to the police will weigh against you. The court
is likely to view them as an attempt to create a straw man of
physical abuse for litigation purposes and, thus, not believe any
of your testimony.

"You could offer your husband the option of moving out voluntarily and a *nonabandonment letter.* This letter would state that
your husband's moving out is without prejudice to future determination of who should exclusively occupy the house or who
should have custody of the children. You can also offer your husband additional *visitation* as inducement for moving out, as well
as exclusive use of the summer home.

"I do not, however, want to hold out too much hope that
your husband will accept this offer. His lawyer will advise him
that the court will look upon his moving out as concession of
custody, no matter what the letter says.

"You face the same problems as your husband if you voluntarily move. Therefore, I cannot advise you to do so. Your problems are not likely to be resolved quickly. Keep working at building your business. Stay active with friends and neighbors. Use
them and your therapist as the basis of a support system."

The Courts and Public Policy

As we have seen, the spouse's therapists recognize that it is in
everyone's emotional interests for one of the parents to move out
of the home. At the same time, their lawyers advise each spouse
to remain in the home so as not to compromise their respective

legal positions in a fault-based divorce state. Although a court is not likely to order either spouse to move, its reasoning differs from that of both the therapists and the attorneys.

What, you may ask, is the conception of public policy that justifies binding the Golds to live together in endless disharmony and deteriorating mental health?

Authorizing a spouse to move from the marital residence is, obviously, a serious determination. The state, through its courts, provides official sanction for what society regards as the actual end of the marriage relationship, even if legal formalities remain. Under the current laws of most states, a court compels one spouse to move from the marital residence only when he or she is indisputably posing a threat to the physical well-being of other members of the family.

At this time, the courts generally do not regard emotional harm as a serious enough basis upon which to make a determination that a spouse should be allowed to leave home. This seems to be out of whack with most other aspects of society, which long ago stopped regarding emotional trauma as being imaginary or insignificant.

Continuous turmoil for parents and children debilitates both their capacity to cope and their productive role in family and society. The courts and the legislature should recognize the need for a legal remedy to relieve the stress and pain of families like the Golds.

Another concern of the court lies in problems of proof. Medical history and records can usually verify physical abuse. In cases like the one in question, however, no such obvious source of verification exists for emotional damage.

The courts may fear that a standard of emotional harm could deteriorate to the point at which it would become a ridiculously simple matter of fabricating trivial claims of psychological anguish. Certainly, credible mental health testimony has to be an essential part of the proof process. But as difficult as such claims can be to prove to a reasonable degree of certainty, this does not justify ignoring them.

An unarticulated conception of the children's best interests may also be the basis of the present rule. A court may believe the

Gold children are better off if their parents live under the same roof, even if they are in a state of perpetual emotional warfare.

This analysis, however, does not consider the child's long-range welfare. While a child may be immediately and severely stressed by the parent's physical separation, that does not mean that in the long run he or she does not benefit. In fact, there is no definitive proof that the quality of life for children whose parents divorce is any better (or worse) than that for children who grow up with two intractable, fighting parents living under the same roof. I suspect that the crucial variable is not whether the parents live together but how they manage their conflicts.

The courts recognize that before Irv or Sue can be authorized to leave the home, the children must be protected. Their interests are best served by a stable custody and support arrangement that ensures them access to both parents' emotional and financial resources—even if one parent lives away from the marital residence.

The parents' agreement to—or the court's imposition of—a carefully constructed custody and support arrangement should be a precondition to authorizing a parent to move.

The courts should pressure emotionally embattled parents and their lawyers to make the children's welfare their first priority. By honoring a moving-out request, the courts could automatically break down the bundle of issues involved in a divorce. Child custody and support and temporary maintenance could be decided first and, thus, separated from property division, permanent maintenance, counsel fees, and grounds for divorce.

Finally, the current rule that makes it difficult for a spouse to leave home may also be explained by a court's fear of altering the balance of negotiating power. If his request to move out is granted with parental rights essentially preserved, Irv would gain a substantial advantage in negotiations. In effect, Irv would have his children, his girlfriend, and a new home free from Sue's presence. Sue, on the other hand, would lose a great deal of leverage, since Irv's incentive to make economic or custody concessions to Sue would be dramatically reduced.

Certainly, the court's setting adequate maintenance and child-support payments should be a prerequisite to permitting Irv to move. Irv must meet his basic economic responsibilities to his wife and children if he wants the right to leave the marital home without penalty.

Assuming the court sets adequate levels of child support and temporary maintenance, the Gold children's welfare should not be a bargaining chip to better the negotiating position of either spouse. Basically, courts are not supposed to be in the business of equalizing resources. Their primary role is to resolve matrimonial disputes while promoting the best interests of the children.

In any case, I would like to offer the following suggestions for reform by the courts and legislature in states in which fault must still be proved to obtain a divorce:

1. (a) Explicitly recognize emotional harm as a basis for allowing one parent to leave the marital home without prejudice; and (b) create an expeditious motion and evaluation procedure to authorize a parent to move out without prejudice to future *modification of custody.*

The purpose of this suggestion is to alleviate the situation wherein parents cannot live together, but at the same time neither can move out without prejudice.

The notion that leaving the marital home is a voluntary agreement for the other spouse to have custody is, at best, a fiction. A parent may want to move out only to preserve his or her own mental health or that of the children. The courts, however, pile fiction upon fiction by giving "priority" in future custody determinations to de facto agreements reached through moving out.

I believe that the parent who seeks the right to move out should be allowed to do so, with the stipulation that he or she must make a preliminary showing detailing the emotional harm he or she and the other family members are suffering. The parent would also be required to provide the court with detailed, realistic plans for custody, child support, and temporary maintenance.

This kind of preliminary showing would, in turn, trigger expeditious investigation by an independent mental health professional whose explicit purpose would be to examine the entire family for emotional harm. Establishment of a panel of independent mental health professionals to do "moving out" assessments would ameliorate the therapists' dilemma of whether to treat or to advocate (more about this on page 172). It would also eliminate the therapists' problem of having to reveal their diagnosis, treatment plan, and confidential communications in an adversarial setting.

Once chosen, a panel professional would be given access to whatever family members he or she deems necessary to complete the assessment. The panel member would then submit a written report and recommendation to the court, including a proposed custody plan. The standard for allowing a parent to move out would be based on the risk of serious emotional harm to one or more family members if the spouses remain under the same roof. If either or both parents oppose the expert's recommendation, the court would then schedule an immediate hearing at which the expert would testify.

2. Routinely appoint an attorney for children in custody disputes.

There are a number of conceptual and practical problems with appointment of an attorney for children enmeshed in a custody dispute. If properly instructed by the court, however, such an attorney can provide useful advocacy on behalf of the children's interests. If nothing else, the attorney can ensure that the moving-out requests stay on a fast track toward resolution.

Some states have a situation whereby an advocate for the children is appointed automatically at state expense. Unfortunately, the great majority of states do not have the money to fund this expensive but well-advised policy. To require divorcing families to pay for yet another lawyer would put the costs of divorce out of most people's reach.

I've spoken with a number of judges about this issue. Some would very much like to see such a measure instituted. Others feel it's unnecessary. Basically, the problem comes down to one of economics. The parties can't afford it, and neither can the states. On one level, that's reality. Still, we have to ask ourselves if we're throwing out the baby with the bathwater.

3. Re-examine the law regarding confidentiality of communications between lawyers and therapists working with a divorcing couple.

In creating interdisciplinary solutions to divorce, it is essential that attorneys and mental health professionals begin opening the lines of communication. Unfortunately, there are some inherent problems in creating such a dialogue. It's only natural for therapists who are treating different family members to be careful about revealing information that can benefit an adversary.

This threat of disclosure makes it difficult for the professionals who serve a client to approach the client's problems in a coordinated manner. That is unfortunate, since full disclosure would serve an important social interest in promoting a court's informed decision making regarding the children's welfare. Nevertheless, our job is to work within the system as it exists—not as we want it to be.

At present, there is no easy answer to how the balance between these competing values should be drawn. I do believe, however, that the question of confidentiality of interprofessional communications concerning common divorcing clients is an area that must be addressed by legal and mental health professionals as well as by the courts if the interdisciplinary approach I envision is to become a reality.

Suggestions for Creating a Productive Relationship between Legal and Mental Health Professionals

Attempting to change the court system would be a Herculean task—far more difficult, even, than trying to change people. Beyond continuing to voice the kind of suggestions I've indicated and working within your state to alter current laws, there is not a great deal more one can do in the short run.

Basically, I think it would be a far better expenditure of time and energy to work at changing individual behavior. Before we come back to the central issues of what Irv and Sue can do to better their situation, let's first look at some steps attorneys and mental health professionals can take to ease the suffering of families like the Golds.

There are two basic prerequisites. First, the members of each profession must understand the outlook of and ethical constraints on the other. Second, each professional also must be willing to communicate within the limits of confidentiality and their professional responsibilities. Let's explore five possible ways this could work in the case at hand:

1. Either of the therapists could ask the client's permission to meet with the attorney. The purpose of the meeting would be to underscore the emotional harm that the client is suffering and to push for immediate resolution.

Attorneys should realize that most therapists have serious concerns about speaking to them. Therapists often do not understand the goals and tactics of their client's attorney and view the attorney with suspicion. Therapists are also concerned about breaching their confidential relationship with clients (though the client's permission to contact the attorney alleviates much of that problem).

To further allay confidentiality concerns, the client should be informed that the discussion between lawyer and therapist took place and should be told the substance of what transpired.

The therapist also worries about complicating the therapeutic relationship. As a result of the therapist's active intervention with the attorney, the client may perceive the therapist as his or her advocate.

One of the principal tools of therapy is the analysis of *transference,* which serves as the basis of the client's response to the therapist. A client transfers onto the therapist his or her feelings about relationships with emotionally significant people in his or her past. Therapists consciously try to foster and not distort transference by attempting to maintain a position of neutrality with their clients.

A client's feelings of obligation to a therapist-turned-advocate may lead to the repression or denial of feelings that may confuse the process of transference, thus undermining the whole therapeutic relationship. The therapist must weigh these risks against the benefit of the lawyer's full understanding of the emotional health of the client. It is possible in some cases that a shift from therapy to advocacy will mean the end of treatment.

The lawyer should welcome a call from a therapist who can address these obstacles. After determining what harm being legally locked in the house is doing to the client and the children, counsel should be willing to reconsider giving advice against moving out.

A conscientious attorney should consider whether there are higher goals than winning a case—such as protecting the welfare of children—and address those issues with the client. At the same time, the attorney also must devise a program to control the legal damage resulting from moving out. As a result of the therapist's call, the lawyer might also explore settlement options more seriously.

2. A joint meeting could take place, with the therapist, the patient, and the lawyer all in attendance, to exchange information and explore alternatives.

3. A meeting of the therapists for Irv, Sue, and the children could be set to assess the harm being done to the family and to recommend a unified course. This meeting raises serious confidentiality concerns because it indisputably places the therapist in the role of an advocate. The participants all have primary allegiances to different parties with adversary interests.

All three therapists, no doubt, have learned confidential information that each might divulge to the other. Each therapist might in turn reveal that confidential information to their respective patients, and might later also have to testify about the discussion at the meeting.

Obviously, a joint meeting should not be organized without explicit consent from all the clients and their attorneys. Advance written agreement to the ground rules for such a meeting is essential.

4. Irv, Sue, or the children's therapist (or all three) might jointly meet with Irv and Sue's attorneys.

5. A meeting could take place with the lawyers, the spouses, and some or all of the therapists in attendance.

Possibilities 4 and 5 depend on the willingness of the spouses to discuss the family crisis with professionals identified with the other side. Confidentiality is, once again, a major concern in such meetings, but one that can at least be partly assuaged by laying down written ground rules in advance.

All of the consultations and conferences should aim at agreement on a stipulation that permits one of the parents to move out and provides for *child custody, child support,* and temporary *maintenance.* The stipulation must explicitly negate prejudice to either party for future applications for modifications of any of its provisions.

No presumption concerning permanent custody arrangements should be made from the stipulation. Issues of property distribution and divorce grounds would be deferred for negotiation at a later date.

Can an Interdisciplinary Approach to Divorce Really Work?

I believe that it is possible for attorneys and mental health professionals to work together in the best interests of a family. Given the way the present system is set up, however, there are still many problems to resolve. We've been exploring some of the tensions between legal and mental health professionals. In addition to the very real issues of confidentiality and conflict of interest, there are also questions of professional training and style.

Every professional has his or her own way of doing business. Lawyers are trained to focus on financial and procedural matters. Unfortunately, many of them are insensitive to their client's emotional needs. I must admit that I've heard more than one practitioner of marital law categorize the entire field of mental health as "that touchy-feely bull."

Attorneys are taught the importance of achieving victory for their clients, but as we've seen, this concept is not so easy to define in a divorce action. I don't expect lawyers to become experts in psychology. Nevertheless, it is time to start looking at clients in the throes of divorce not only as people but as people who are going through one of the most devastating experiences of their lives.

At the same time, I have seen counselors and psychotherapists so caught up with their client's emotional concerns that they completely fail to grasp key legal and financial issues that come into play. Furthermore, some mental health people have such a negative predisposition to attorneys that they would never even consider working cooperatively.

I feel that it is no longer productive for professionals who must deal with the same clients to work at cross-purposes, even if the law does, to some extent, dictate such an approach.

Dr. Sylvan Schaffer, as both a psychotherapist and an attorney, has looked at divorce from an unusually broad perspective. In considering the problems of collaborating in a family's best interests, Dr. Schaffer feels that, in general, attorneys shoulder more of the blame than do counselors and psychotherapists.

"Attorneys tend to keep the concept of winning in mind, from the point of view of their particular client rather than in terms of the whole family. That's why therapists and counselors are in a far better position than lawyers to consider the interests of all the parties involved.

"A therapist can legitimately say to a client that, if one looks at the whole picture, the children would be better off with the other spouse. It is a rare attorney, indeed, who would suggest something like that.

"Basically, the attorney looks at the case in terms of winning for his client, while the therapist is more interested in the emerging mental health picture. The same goes for custody. The issue for the attorney is winning for the client, while the therapist sees it in terms of what is best for the child.

"For the most part, it is the attorneys who are into playing power games. Lawyers are the ones with adversarial agendas, not therapists. Therefore, it is really in the ballpark of the attorneys as to how they treat therapists, who by and large do not have that adversarial bent. Therapists understand that their primary role is to care for their patients.

"In fact, many therapists hate getting involved in heavily contested divorce cases because they resent being manipulated by a couple of contentious lawyers. I get calls all the time from therapists who say: 'Please save me! I'm getting subpoenas. I'm being harassed. Is there any way to get out of this?'

"That's why I feel strongly that if an interdisciplinary approach to divorce is ever really going to work, it's up to attorneys to start changing the ground rules."

Basically, I have no quarrel with Dr. Schaffer's criticism of attorneys, but there are those of us who are actively involved in initiating a dialogue with therapists. I recognize that my primary role is to act as an advocate on behalf of my clients, but I do try my best to deal with the whole person—and his or her long-term concerns.

Furthermore, I am not enamored with the notion of psychotherapists avoiding contentious divorce cases because they don't provide a particularly comfortable ambience. Certainly it isn't easy to put yourself in the middle of a war, but—as the saying goes—somebody has to do it!

If I were primarily interested in peace and quiet, I could find other more suitable areas of law. Any counselor or therapist who is truly dedicated to helping families survive divorce must be prepared to enter the battlefield.

Despite all the apparent problems, I'm optimistic that in the coming years we will see more and more cooperation between legal and mental health professionals. The American Academy of Matrimonial Lawyers (N.Y. Chapter) has taken the lead in this area. They have established a coordinating group of legal and mental health organizations—the Interdisciplinary Forum of Mental Health and Family Law—that Rona Shays, Esq. and I have cochaired since its founding in 1986. Thus, I see positive movement in that direction. Granted, there are many issues yet to be resolved; nevertheless, I am encouraged about the future.

I've heard it said that mixing an attorney and a therapist in a divorce case is akin to combining oil and water, but I take a different view. Ten years ago, there was virtually no dialogue between the professions. Today, one sees any number of interdisciplinary conferences and collaborations. Naturally, the question is whether real communication and cooperation can take place in the heat of battle. Again, I'm optimistic.

Before they can have communication and cooperative effort, people must have some understanding of one another's viewpoint. In the past few years, I have witnessed a great deal of progress in this area.

I have received calls and letters from lawyers and mental health people throughout the country who are interested in starting interdisciplinary groups in their states. Some of them have read or heard about the presentations my colleagues and I have made at meetings of the American Bar Association, the American Psychological Association, the American Academy of Child and Adolescent Psychiatry, and at many other meetings of prestigious legal and mental health organizations—and want to know more about the concept. Once again, I am proud to say that the American Academy of Matrimonial Lawyers, of which I am a Fellow, is taking the lead in this area on a national level. To me, this bodes well for the future of a true interdisciplinary approach to divorce that will benefit the client experiencing the anguish of divorce.

Can You Really Win?

I think I can anticipate a question that many of you have on your minds: "All this stuff about increased professional cooperation is well and good, but how is it going to help me solve the many problems I'm forced to deal with right now?"

For one thing, there are important analogies between the dynamics of professional and personal communication. Certainly, attorneys and therapists have conflicting goals on certain levels. Nevertheless, both have an ethical obligation to consider the welfare of the client. Believe me, I get no satisfaction from winning an economic battle on behalf of a client if it causes his or her life to become more stressful.

Spouses who are undergoing separation or divorce also have some common goals to consider. If there are children involved, such as in the case of the Gold family, that should be more than reason enough to keep some lines of communication open.

As in most divorcing families, the Gold children are truly the tragic figures in the story. Despite the genuine love both parents feel, they have fallen into the common trap of using the children as pawns in the divorce war. I realize that it isn't easy to avoid the temptation to fight over your children as if they were possessions. Still, a loving parent has an obligation to place a child's best interests above his or her own.

"If you really love someone," observes Dr. Sylvan Schaffer, "you can give them up if it is necessary. When you view a child as a possession, that is not a definition of love.

"I think that every parent should be required to read the Book of Kings in the Bible. When King Solomon had a custody case to decide, he would order the child cut in half. The parent who viewed the child as chattel would be willing to see him slaughtered before forgoing their half-share. But the truly loving parent would invariably say, 'I will give up my child, rather than let him be hurt.' This was the sole basis on which Solomon rendered his custody judgment."

I realize that we are almost in the twenty-first century. Still, there is much to be said for the approach of that wise old king. I believe that divorcing parents have it in their power to spare their children a tremendous amount of anguish. I'm not saying it's easy, but it can be done. Two separating or divorcing spouses can sit down and make a rational decision not to let their war wreak havoc upon innocent children—their children!

Now, I am not suggesting to those who insist upon it that this would necessarily exclude having a good old-fashioned knock-down, drag-out economic fight. You can still do that, while trying to separate the issues relative to the children, such as *child custody* and *visitation.*

Basically, two people have it in their power to structure any kind of divorce they want. Virtually everything we've discussed regarding problems dealing with attorneys and therapists can be nullified by spouses who truly understand the meaning of winning. I've said it before, but I think it's worth repeating:

The only way to emerge a winner is to position yourself as the person in control—the captain of your ship. Lawyers and therapists are people who work for you, professionals whose job it is, within the bounds of professional ethics and judgment, to help you achieve your goals. If one or more of the professionals isn't doing his or her job, consider replacing that person and hiring someone else.

Instead of depending on your attorney or therapist to make decisions and value judgments for you, try to use them to help you acquire as much self-knowledge and relevant information as possible. Then, set some positive short- and long-term goals and start working at the business of making your life happier and more fulfilling.

Please don't get me wrong. It is not my intention to make this sound simpler than it actually is. It takes hard work and determination to define your goals and empower yourself to shape your own future, especially when you are going through this terrible upheaval in your life.

To make matters worse, you may find that your spouse is working at cross-purposes, making your life more difficult and miserable every step of the way. Even so, it is possible to overcome that adversity by staying aware and doing your best to control those things that are within your power.

I've seen spouses remain rational, even when the other is acting inappropriately, seeking only victory and revenge. Moreover, there are mothers and fathers who simply won't get into negativity and mind games because of the adverse effect it might have on the children.

In any case, it is you who must maintain a handle on the proceedings, even though this is a tall order in the midst of such a heavy crisis. I can see no other solution—no other way to win.

As someone who is on the front lines of the divorce wars day after day, I've seen just about every kind of scenario. It is my hope that by giving you a complete picture of what is involved, you will be able to come out of this process relatively unscathed. In the final analysis, that will depend on your willingness to take matters in your own hands and to make positive choices under adverse conditions.

Remember: It's not going to be a particularly straight or easy road, but if you stick to it, with a vision for the future, you will greatly enhance your prospects for emerging as a winner.

11

Advantages and Drawbacks of a Collaborative Divorce

I've been talking a great deal about how important it is for divorcing couples to take matters into their own hands. Let's look at three basic settlement scenarios and how they tie in with controlling your own destiny.

1. Litigation: Settlement reached by court decision
2. Negotiation: Settlement reached by the parties through their attorneys
3. Collaborative alternatives

Litigation: Settlement Reached by Court Decision

Husbands and wives in the throes of divorce sometimes become so enraged that they act against their own self-interest. And believe me, that's what going to court comes down to in most cases.

By the time a case goes before a judge, all other options should have either failed or have been eliminated. Presumably, the parties and their attorneys have not been able to reach mutually acceptable terms regarding finances and child-related issues.

As I've pointed out earlier, less than 10 percent of all divorce cases are resolved in court. Those that are tend to be the ones that are most bitterly contested. Court is where you are most likely to find couples who deal in scorched earth—spouses more obsessed with revenge than any other factor. They don't care that this dragged-out fight is hurting the children or that it is draining them financially.

The legal fees in such bitterly contested divorces can reach astronomical proportions. If you factor in the cost of the appraisers that are retained to evaluate the marital property and the mental health experts to testify to the relative emotional fitness of a husband or wife in a custody battle, except for the very wealthy, a grim picture of long-term financial devastation begins to emerge.

Now, the monetary cost of all this is horrific enough. Nevertheless, it is not the worst aspect of taking your divorce before a judge. To my mind, the most inhibiting factor is the uncertainty of the outcome. You and your attorney may believe that you've proved your case, but a judge might not see it that way—for a raft of reasons.

First, many of our divorce laws are still evolving and are thus subject to varying interpretations. Also, the mores of our society have been shifting with far greater speed than the laws or public policy. Finally, there are the frailties and biases of the judges themselves, who are, after all, as human as the rest of us.

Unless you're out to start World War III, you'll probably want to get your divorce over with as quickly and inexpensively as possible. If this is your goal, I repeat: try to settle the case rather than going to court!

Negotiation: Settlement Reached by the Parties Through Their Attorneys

It is ironic that although the vast majority of divorcing spouses will not wind up in front of a judge, it behooves the parties and their attorneys to proceed as if this were not the case. In effect, virtually all divorce negotiations take place in the shadow of the courthouse.

Once divorce seems like a certainty, your attorney will proceed as if you're going to trial—even though he or she knows in advance that this will almost definitely not come to pass. Nevertheless, attorneys will go through the mechanics for two basic reasons:

- To gather information relevant to the case.
- To establish a strong negotiating position by demonstrating to the other side that you are, indeed, serious about going to court if necessary.

More often than not, a settlement between the parties will be reached out of court. At that point, the attorneys will draw up a settlement agreement and submit it to a judge. While I can predict with relative certainty that the terms of divorce will, for the vast majority of couples, be settled out of court, it is far more difficult to answer the two basic questions that are foremost on the minds of new clients: How long is this process going to take? How much money will it cost?

I've had clients tell me that their spouse is eager to resolve things without bitterness, only to find instead that he or she intends to wage a full-scale war. In some cases, the new client has simply misread the situation. Or perhaps, upon reflection, the spouse has had a change of heart. Then again, the problem may stem from a particularly contentious attorney goading a client who would otherwise be far more conciliatory. In any event, it usually takes a while to assess the approach and predisposition of the other side.

In addition, a certain amount of time is required before an attorney can ascertain what kind of problems he or she is going to have in the evaluation of assets and can determine how those assets will be divided. In the meantime, most attorneys proceed with the legal mechanics as outlined in chapter 9.

Once both parties have made a complete financial disclosure, most rational clients will ask their attorneys: "When can you start negotiating?" Assuming that revenge and vindication are not the primary motivating factors, the vast majority of husbands and wives will be eager to sit down and start resolving matters as soon as possible.

At some point, it is thus possible to start negotiating with an eye toward an agreement. This assumes that you have rational counsel on both sides—professionals who are not trying to drag things out in order to bolster their egos or fees.

While I have encountered irrational positions by counsel more often than I'd care to remember, that is not the way negotiations between two competent and concerned attorneys usually transpire. In most cases, the kind of response I'll get is: "Tell me what you're looking for. Make me an offer I can't refuse, and maybe we can put this case to bed."

At that point, you can begin meaningful settlement discussions. Perhaps, at the same time, the spouses may also be talking to each other about resolving outstanding disputes. To my mind, the main requirement for success is the spirit in which negotiations take place. As with any other process, negotiations between lawyers have their share of risks and limitations. Indeed, the very phrase, "adversarial divorce," can conjure up images of endless and unimaginably expensive legal battles.

Undeniably, such nightmares do occur. Still, our system of justice is based on an adversarial system—with each side represented by competent counsel. If all parties are reasonable and so disposed, a negotiated divorce can be a desirable approach. Then again, there are all kinds of negotiations.

There is cooperative negotiation, where both parties and counsel sit down and talk amicably, with an eye toward resolving conflicts in a mutually satisfactory manner. On the other hand, some people choose to play hardball, and that's a whole different kind of animal.

People who are not negotiating in good faith will do anything to manipulate the balance of power in their favor. All kinds of subtle (and not so subtle) forms of pressure can enter into the picture, including when a spouse doesn't pay *maintenance* or *child support* or when he or she violates preexisting *visitation* or *child custody* arrangements. Those are all forms of negotiation—albeit spiteful ones. Attorneys can exacerbate this bitter game by unduly and unnecessarily prolonging the process of pretrial *discovery* or by excessive *motion practice*.

In the end, I believe that the fault lies not with the adversarial system itself so much as with the estranged spouses and attorneys who misuse it. As we will see, no form of conflict settlement is perfect or immune to the abuses of those who are determined to exploit it.

Collaborative Alternatives to a Contested Divorce

The whole notion of collaborative divorce strikes some people as being a contradiction in terms. This is an understandable response. We have all seen any number of bitter divorces dragged through the media. There are, of course, more than enough contentious marital breakups in the real world as well. Nevertheless, it doesn't have to be that way.

There are a growing number of cases in which people decide to divorce by mutual consent. Even when there is a rejector and a rejectee, some spouses can eventually come to terms with the reality that their marriage is over. At that point, they can make a rational decision to approach divorce as a joint venture.

Is this far-fetched? Perhaps so, for couples who never had any communication in the first place and are filled with hate. But let's go back to our analogy of the partnership of marriage as a business enterprise.

If two business partners decide that they want to go their separate ways, would this constitute a declaration of war? Not necessarily. People have a right to change their minds about continuing any kind of collaboration—and that includes marriage.

I fully realize that the partnership of marriage involves ethical and moral commitments that go far beyond those in a business relationship. Indeed, our wedding vows include the phrases, "for better or for worse," and "till death do us part." For couples with children, there is an even greater obligation to work at maintaining a cohesive family. Nevertheless, divorce has become a fact of life in our culture. As distasteful as this reality might be, as harmful as broken marriages are to society, as symbolic as the divorce phenomenon may be of the confused and morally impoverished age in which we live—it has become part of the fabric of our lives.

Once a man and woman decide that their marriage is irretrievably broken, the issue then becomes one of proceeding with
the divorce in the most expedient and constructive way possible.
We have seen why a protracted court battle rarely serves a useful
purpose. For most couples, the real choice comes down to proceeding with a traditional divorce or opting for an arbitrated or
mediated settlement.

ARBITRATION

Arbitration is a method that can be employed between the parties
to resolve a specific issue, a series of issues, or all of the issues.
It is, in many respects, similar to the kind of conflict resolution
that has been used in labor disputes. In business contracts, there
is often a clause stipulating that disputes will be submitted to an
arbitrator, whose decision will be binding on both parties.

The purpose of *arbitration* in these contexts, as in divorce, is
to avoid a lengthy and more costly court battle. Let me give you
an anecdotal example of how this process works:

Bill and Fran are in the process of divorcing. Most of the
issues are settled, but they and their lawyers cannot reach an
agreement about the length and amount of *maintenance* Bill
should be required to pay.

Fran wants to receive a thousand dollars a month for five
years. Bill wants to pay five hundred dollars for two years. Several months have gone by, and there is no movement on either
side. Husband and wife agree that they have reached a stale-
mate. Counsel has been cooperative, but the parties just can't
resolve this problem. Rather than take this matter before a
judge, the parties prefer a more informal proceeding. Both attorneys agree that arbitration would be appropriate.

Bill and Fran formally agree that this dispute will be submitted to an arbitrator and that his or her decision will be binding.
That decision, in turn, will then be entered in as part of the *separation agreement* or *judgment* of divorce.

At that point, the parties and their attorneys appear before
a mutually acceptable arbitrator. Each side informally submits its
position. Then, the arbitrator renders a decision—one way or

the other. While the scope of arbitration tends to be limited, the process does have certain clear advantages over a court trial.

In an arbitration, the parties get to choose their arbitrator or at least have a veto over possible choices. In judicial proceedings, however, a judge is assigned by the court. Furthermore, the arbitration process tends to be faster and far more informal. Meetings are held in private, and arbitrators are not bound by the same rules of evidence as are judges.

More states are considering arbitration as a less expensive and less time-consuming way to decide property issues between divorcing spouses. Nevertheless, this option is not nearly as popular or comprehensive a method of conflict resolution in divorce cases as the next process we will examine.

MEDIATION

Arbitration does not constitute a true collaborative divorce, in the sense that the decision making is left to the arbitrator. In *mediation,* however, the divorcing parties are responsible for hammering out their own agreement with the help of a mediator. This is a process that affords two people the opportunity to end a marriage on their own terms.

If you want to avoid the bias of a judge, the ambiguity of the laws, and a contentious battle between attorneys, *mediation* might be the way to go. Despite its advantages, however, mediation is not for everyone. Nor is it without its problems and limitations. But before we get into those, let's look at what the mediation process entails.

In a divorce mediation, a neutral and trained third party helps the disputing spouses arrive at a mutually acceptable final settlement of their own design. In general, agreements made during the mediation are embodied in a *memorandum of understanding,* which is then incorporated into the final divorce agreement.

Unlike an arbitrator, a mediator has no decision-making powers. Furthermore, he or she cannot compel the parties to accept a particular settlement—or even to continue mediating their differences. No matter how good the mediator, his or her role is essentially that of a facilitator. Because the decision-making process is put squarely on the shoulders of the divorcing spouses, mediation requires a strong commitment on both their parts. For this reason, most experienced mediators require the parties to sign a formal agreement spelling out the basic ground rules. These might include the following:

- A statement of the issues subject to mediation.
- A statement to the effect that, although the mediator has a genuine concern for both parties and their children, he or she does not represent either side.
- Acknowledgment that all participation in the mediation process is voluntary. Thus, the mediator will not permit either side to blame, abuse, or exert pressure on the other in an attempt to assert his or her will.
- Acknowledgment that the voluntary nature of the mediation process gives both parties—and the mediator—complete freedom to unilaterally withdraw from the proceedings at any time.
- While the confidentiality of mediations is not mandated by law, most experienced mediators will insist that all discussions and their subsequent outcomes be privileged. In the event that the mediation does not produce a mutually acceptable agreement, none of the discussions or revelations that surface during the sessions can be used in court.
- In order to maintain impartiality, the mediator declares that he or she cannot be called as a witness to testify in any subsequent legal action regarding issues discussed during the mediation.
- While the mediator may choose to provide limited amounts of specific information, he or she will not be offering legal advice of any kind.
- Any economic agreement must be based on a full financial disclosure by both parties.
- Both spouses are free to and are encouraged to seek the counsel of lawyers and other professionals.

- A specific date is set on which the mediation process will terminate.

When a couple agrees to mediate their differences, they implicitly express a willingness to attempt to resolve their disputes in a manner that is both positive and collaborative. This is no easy task for the vast majority of divorcing couples.

Even those spouses who are still on relatively good terms may view one another with a certain amount of distrust and suspicion. In reality, most couples who turn to mediation do so not so much as an act of good faith but because they perceive it as being the lesser evil.

When a husband and wife enter into mediation, they implicitly agree to replace their lack of trust in one another with a mutual confidence in the mediator's ability to help them reach a fair and mutually acceptable agreement. Initially, the parties must grant the mediator the power to manage the communications during the sessions.

As negotiations progress, the parties should learn to acknowledge one another's needs. In time, both spouses come to realize that, despite their conflicts, they still have many common interests.

Since a great many couples who opt for mediation are those with dependent children, the idea of common interests is by no means an abstraction. If children of divorce are going to survive and thrive, they are going to need the ongoing love and support of both parents. This will require constant communication between an estranged mother and father.

When couples divorce, they are often at a low point in their ability to communicate. A skilled mediator can help both parties establish a level of understanding and trust that they may never have achieved during their marriage. As negotiations progress, the mediator tries to return an increasing amount of control to the parties.

By the time an agreement is hammered out, both spouses should feel satisfied with the outcome and be able to move forward on that basis. A good mediator understands that the mediation process can have great value as a learning experience.

He or she tries to create a climate in which the improved communication and negotiation skills developed in the mediation process can carry over into the couple's ongoing interaction—particularly in relation to the children.

The steps entailed in a successful mediation can be divided into three phases, and summarized as follows:

Phase 1:

- Husband and wife agree to negotiate in good faith in hopes of achieving a mutually acceptable agreement.
- Both parties interview and eventually agree upon the selection of a mediator.
- Both parties agree on the issues that will be resolved in the process and sign an agreement drawn up by the mediator that spells out the ground rules.

Phase 2:

- The mediator works with the spouses to create a climate in which husband and wife both feel free to express their respective points of view.
- Each party learns to hear and acknowledge the other's wants and needs.
- The spouses begin to understand and respect the differences between their separate and common interests.
- Both parties become more interested in a collaborative solution than in their own self-serving agendas.

Phase 3:

- The parties reach a mutually acceptable agreement that is reviewed by their respective attorneys.
- Both spouses feel a long-term commitment to live up to the letter and spirit of the agreement.

Now, you may be wondering why all divorcing couples don't opt for mediation. Based on the above description, it seems like a benign and constructive solution to a difficult situation. As you will see, however, mediation may not be the best solution for you. Furthermore, even those couples who might be well-served by mediation ought to be aware of its inherent dangers and limitations.

Difficulties in Finding a Qualified Mediator. At this juncture, no state licenses divorce mediators. Most good mediators are attorneys, mental health professionals, and others skilled in conflict resolution. At the same time, however, anyone, even without any qualification or training, can call themselves a mediator. Indeed, some couples use unqualified personal friends to serve this function. While I understand the temptation to involve someone husband and wife both know and trust, using an inexperienced or untrained mediator can have disastrous consequences.

I strongly advise you to consider using only divorce mediators who have training and experience in one or more of the following areas:

- Conflict resolution and management.
- Theory and practice of mediation, specifically divorce mediation.
- Emotional and psychological aspects of divorce pertaining to both parents and children.
- Financial and legal ramifications of divorce.

Keep in mind that mediators are not licensed or regulated by any governing body that requires a specific code of ethics or standards. Unlike attorneys and mental health professionals, they cannot be disciplined for improper professional behavior.

Fortunately, there are some good mediators out there, but it will take a lot of research to find them. Your attorney or therapist may be able to refer you to qualified people in your area. There are also organizations, such as the Family Mediation Association in Bethesda, Maryland, that can provide you with the names of qualified mediators in your state.

Before you select a mediator, I suggest that you interview several. Ask about their experience, the kinds of cases they've worked on, and their knowledge of current divorce law. I've prepared a short checklist to help you in your search. Use it to interview mediators and to evaluate to what extent they merit your consideration.

Is This the Right Mediator for Me?

1. How did I contact this person?

2. What is the mediator's primary field of expertise?

3. How much previous experience does the mediator have— particularly in divorce cases?

4. How much specific training does this person have in the area of divorce mediation?

5. How many divorce or custody cases has the person mediated in the past year?

6. Is this person a member of any national or statewide mediation groups?

7. What are this person's feelings about working with attorneys, mental health professionals, and accountants to resolve particular issues?

8. Does the mediator have any biases that might influence the settlement?

9. Does the mediator believe in maintaining complete confidentiality?

10. How much does the mediator charge for his or her services?

By the time you have interviewed three or four mediators, you will get a feel for their respective personal and professional styles. Remember that your spouse will also want to interview people, so you will have to make a mutual decision about who is the best person with whom to work.

If you follow the guidelines I've just outlined, you and your spouse should be able to find a qualified mediator. Nevertheless, I would like you to consider some other reasons why mediation may not be the best solution for you.

Disadvantages and Dangers of Mediation. You'll notice that question 8 on the checklist refers to the possibility of bias on the part of a mediator. Unlike most of the other questions, impartiality is not a particularly comfortable subject to broach with someone whose job it is to remain neutral. You may, however, want to inquire about the prospective mediator's personal background.

Has he or she been through one or more divorces? How were financial and child custody issues resolved? Does he or she lean toward any particular formula for deciding these matters?

By encouraging mediators to discuss such delicate issues, you can gain a great deal of insight. Still, there are some patterns of bias that may not surface until you are well into the negotiations. Perhaps you remind the mediator of someone in his or her past. Depending on what feelings that association provokes, you may unknowingly be at a distinct disadvantage.

Now, the same question of bias can justifiably be asked of any attorney whom you might hire as an advocate. For example, I find that lawyers who themselves have gone through a divorce sometimes project their own personal experience onto their clients. This should come as no surprise. Attorneys, mediators, psychotherapists, and judges are all human beings and are, therefore, vulnerable to the foibles and frailties that particular state entails.

Whatever their inner feelings may be about a particular client, however, attorneys are trained and paid to be advocates. Perhaps you've seen news stories about cases in which counsel have defended particularly heinous criminals and asked yourself: "How can they be advocates for such monsters?" The answer is simply that attorneys must fulfill the obligation of their profession as well as an important role in our system of justice.

I must admit that I have represented clients who were, to my way of thinking, far less sympathetic than their estranged spouses. Nevertheless, my course as an advocate is clear. The client's interest is my priority.

With all due respect to mediators, true impartiality can be problematic, to say the least. Let's take a hypothetical case, one that is frequently used to demonstrate this particular limitation in the mediation process.

By definition, the mediator's role is to find a meeting ground between husband and wife. But what happens if, for example, the husband has a far more aggressive and dominating personality than the wife? Where is that magical meeting between an apparent bully and his victim? If the husband is subtle in his domination, a mediator may inadvertently be drawn to the more powerful polarity. On the other hand, the husband's domination may be little more than a show on his part. In reality, he may be a rejectee who is covering up his hurt with an outward display of macho bluster. A less astute mediator may misperceive the situation and be overly partial to the wife.

Now, if negotiations for both spouses in this example were in the hands of two attorneys of relatively equal skill, there would be a more even balance of power. As a rule, the weaker or less dominant spouse stands to gain the most by having his or her rights protected by a strong advocate. When a good attorney is navigating on your behalf, you are less vulnerable to bullying tactics and far less likely to settle for terms that are not in your best interest.

It is ironic that one of the weaknesses of mediation sometimes surfaces because of the mediator's obligation to promote fairness. Let's say you want a 50 percent equity in the family home. As far as you're concerned, that issue is nonnegotiable. Your attorney may well support you on that position if he or she believes it is well-advised. A mediator, on the other hand, would be more likely to encourage a compromise, if only to preserve the trust of both spouses and maintain a climate of fairness.

A further substantial problem relates to the complexities of the issues to be addressed—particularly the financial aspects. As we discussed earlier, experienced counsel is necessary except in the simplest divorce. No less can be said for a mediator. It is difficult, however, to find mediators sufficiently experienced in the financial ramifications. The mediator's lack of training or knowledge may work to your substantial detriment. Thus, it is often important that the mediator be an attorney—or if it is a team—that one be an attorney and the other a mental health professional.

While some critics of mediation point to the difficulties of maintaining a genuinely fair proceeding, there are those who believe that the popularity of this form of conflict resolution is symptomatic of an unfair sexist backlash in the legal system. It has been suggested that, while wives agree to mediate as an attempt to reduce friction, many husbands favor mediation as a way of battering their wives without the interference of a lawyer.

The concept of mediation is based on establishing and maintaining a balance of negotiating power between the parties. Still, some observers point out that in spite of the inroads made by women in recent decades, men continue to wield far greater economic and social power in our society.

The popularity of divorce mediation coincided with the time that women began receiving a more equitable share of the marital pie and increased protection against failure to pay child support. Moreover, a growing number of states have instituted mandatory mediation, particularly as it relates to child custody and visitation issues.

Some observers wonder if this trend toward mediated divorce is a ploy by a male-dominated system to reverse the increased legal and financial protections it has taken women so long to win.

To support the growing imbalance between men and women in this era of mediation and in no-fault divorce, some women's rights advocates point to studies that demonstrate a significant improvement in the living standard of divorced husbands, accompanied by a disproportionate downturn in the economic lifestyles of divorced wives.

While there is no denying a certain amount of sexual bias in certain divorce proceedings, I don't believe that wives should reject the mediation option out of hand. As I pointed out earlier, mediation is not the best option for every couple. Still, it does have some definite advantages, especially when children are involved.

Given two parties who are truly ready to proceed with a collaborative divorce—and the presence of a good mediator—there is much to be said in favor of this option.

When it's handled right, mediation can reduce the emotional trauma of divorce. Furthermore, two people who feel empowered in structuring their own agreement come out of the breakup with a greater sense of self-esteem and a feeling of control over their lives. Under such positive and cooperative circumstances, they are more likely to honor the terms of the divorce settlement.

Now that you've had an opportunity to consider some of the advantages and pitfalls of mediation, you might want to spend a few minutes answering the following questions. While this is not meant to be used as your sole decision-making tool for choosing a collaborative versus an adversarial approach, it will give you some idea of whether the mediation option is one to which you should give serious consideration.

Is Mediation Right for You?

1. What issues remain to be resolved?
2. Are you on relatively cordial terms with your spouse?
3. Do you feel that you and your spouse can be fair-minded for the sake of your and your children's long-range interests?
4. Will you be able to trust your spouse to live up to a collaborative agreement of your own design?
5. Do you honestly trust yourself to live up to an agreement of your own design?
6. Can you work with your spouse in selecting a mutually acceptable mediator?
7. Does your attorney feel that mediation is a viable option in this case?
8. Will you be able to trust the mediator to be fair to both sides?
9. Will you be comfortable with a process that emphasizes cooperation and compromise rather than winning or losing?
10. Do you believe that your spouse can accept a process that emphasizes cooperation and compromise rather than winning or losing?

If you and your spouse can honestly answer "yes" to most of these questions, you may be good candidates for mediation. Should you decide to employ this option, you and your spouse would still require the services of separate counsel. Nevertheless, the attorney's function is somewhat different than it would be in other circumstances. Let's look at some of those differences.

The Attorney's Role in a Mediated Divorce. One of the reasons couples opt for mediation is to avoid a long and expensive battle between two contentious lawyers. Although such fears are understandable, most scorched-earth divorces are perpetuated by the parties, not their attorneys. In any case, the decision to mediate your differences is a sign that you and your spouse are ready to cooperate.

While an attorney plays a far more active role in a litigated or traditional out-of-court divorce, you will still need the help and support of counsel to get the most out of mediation.

Initially, your lawyer will be able to help you determine if mediation is a viable option. If so, he or she can probably recommend some qualified mediators. As the sessions progress, you should consult regularly with your attorney in order to assess the legal and financial ramifications of any and all proposals. In addition, your attorney will want to make certain that all appropriate issues are being discussed. At the very least, it is essential that you don't sign any documents until your attorney has had ample opportunity to examine them.

While an experienced and knowledgeable mediator can help a couple arrive at creative solutions to their problems, he or she must maintain an impartial stance. Remember, even if you work with a mediator who is an attorney, he or she should not offer legal advice. For that, you will need discussions with your own separate counsel. As you and your spouse progress in the mediation process, your attorney still can function as an advocate— by advising you of your rights and the financial and legal consequences of any settlement you might negotiate.

To some extent, the attorney's role in a mediation is not unlike that of a teacher or coach. As negotiations progress and agreements are reached, the attorneys have an obligation not to undermine their clients' decisions. Still, as much as I like to see people take matters into their own hands, I find it difficult to condone terms that go against a client's long-term interests.

As an attorney, it is never easy for me to put the legal and financial interests of my clients on the back burner. Thus, I will make certain that my clients understand the implications of what they are doing—but leave the decision up to them.

Understanding Your Role in the Negotiation Process. Whether you opt for a mediated divorce or for one that is handled by attorneys, you owe it to yourself to take an active interest in the proceedings. There are any number of books that outline the basic principles of negotiation. One that I often recommend is *Getting To Yes,* by Roger Fisher and William Ury. Among other things, the authors stress the importance of four general principles of negotiation, which can be summarized as follows:

- Separating personalities from problems.
- Focusing on common interests rather than polarized positions.
- Expanding the options for mutually acceptable solutions.
- Using objective criteria to make determinations.

In order to use these negotiating skills effectively, it is important that you are aware of your and your spouse's priorities in a divorce settlement. Before you enter into a mediation or your attorney begins substantive discussions, you both should know as many relevant facts about your case as are available.

The importance of timing is something that underlies every negotiation. In the case of divorce, you and your attorney should be moving toward as quick a resolution as possible—especially if children are involved. At the same time, you do not want your spouse to feel that you are in such a hurry to resolve matters that you are willing to compromise on major issues.

As with most of the complex questions that relate to divorce, there are no magic pills or sure-shot solutions. Nevertheless, as you progress in your reading, you will continue to learn more about your options and the importance of making positive and clear-headed decisions. In no area will these skills and strengths be more important than in the way you and your spouse resolve those matters that relate to the care of your children. Not coincidentally, this happens to be the subject of this book's final chapter.

12

Custody and Visitation: Protecting the Children

I N the heat of a divorce battle, two people who are basically rational often lose touch with the things that should matter most—their children. Estranged spouses tend to forget that, although they may choose to become ex-marriage partners, children have no ex-mothers or ex-fathers. Once a husband and wife make the decision to divorce, they must face the fact that they will always be partners in terms of their children, and they should act responsibly and appropriately. Unfortunately, that's often easier said than done.

Most divorcing parents love their children and genuinely do not want to hurt them. Nevertheless, too many estranged husbands and wives are so bent on revenge that they quickly forget their vows not to include innocent children in their quest for victory and vindication.

In most cases, divorce wars are waged over two basic issues—property and custody of the children. As a therapist friend recently noted, "What else are couples going to fight over when their marriage breaks up?"

I realize how easy it is to fall into the trap of battling over your kids as if they were just another possession—albeit a very precious one. Perhaps people are misled by the legal terms that are used in regard to children of divorce. Words like *custody* and *visitation* sound as if one is discussing the fate of prisoners—not innocent children who are, after all, the real casualties of the divorce war. I find that it is far more productive for parents and their attorneys to talk in terms of relative contact with and responsibilities for the children.

You would be well-advised to do all you can to keep concerns about property and children completely separate. I've seen too many couples allow these two issues to mix and mingle in the same unsavory pot. To my mind, this is one of the worst mistakes two divorcing parents can make.

Adults are often unaware that divorce is the saddest experience a child can endure—usually even sadder than the death of a parent. When a child's mother or father dies, there is eventually a sense of closure and usually an understanding of life's inevitable course.

Divorce, on the other hand, presents a far more confusing situation for a young person. The parents are no longer together, yet they are both alive and, in most cases, still physically present in the child's life. Basically, the way children handle this difficult and complicated situation depends on how the parents conduct themselves during and after the divorce.

Studies have shown that children of divorced parents who express ongoing hostility and bitterness toward one another are far more likely to suffer severe depression, become dependent on drugs, or commit suicide. On the other hand, children of parents who manage their divorce rationally and make the children's needs and welfare their priority are better able to avoid major developmental and emotional problems.

Let me ask you a frank question: Do you need any further motivation to seek a nonconfrontational method of resolving arrangements pertaining to your children?

As I've explained, a litigated custody battle can take years to resolve, and since an older child's preference may influence a judge, estranged mothers and fathers often find themselves entering into a bitter competition for the child's affections—using such destructive techniques as brainwashing and bribery.

Examples of brainwashing include one parent saying disparaging things about the other, while extolling the benefits of his or her own case. A mother might chide, "Wouldn't you rather live in this beautiful house with me, instead of that dingy little apartment your father lives in?"

"Is your mom still seeing that same man?" an estranged father might ask provocatively. "Watch out for him. There's something weird about that guy I don't trust."

Bribery of a child is another manipulative tactic that can be expressed in a variety of forms. A parent may be excessively permissive or shower the child with inappropriately expensive gifts. When the child misbehaves, the parent may excuse the most outrageous conduct for fear of losing this ally in a bitter divorce war.

Many estranged parents play these and other destructive psychological games without understanding that they are placing their children's long-term emotional health in serious jeopardy.

If you are going to heed only one piece of advice in this book, I appeal to you to consider the effect that your unthinking actions in the heat of battle can have on your children. Always keep in mind that even though your divorce might be your worst ordeal, it is a far more devastating experience for your children—especially if they are still in their tender years.

A truly loving and thoughtful parent intuitively recognizes the harm that drawn-out custody litigation can wreak. I have even seen some mothers and fathers surrender physical custody to the other parent in order to spare the children the potential consequences of a protracted legal battle.

While I am not suggesting that you compromise your rights, I urge you to take great care in the way you and your spouse resolve matters pertaining to your children. It is worth making the extra effort to work collaboratively for their sake. In view of long-term emotional consequences, this may be the single most important thing you can do to emerge a winner.

Here is a golden opportunity for you to start taking control—not only of the divorce process, but of the ultimate direction your life will take. Maybe your marriage didn't work out, but that's far from the end of the story. Things will get better when you start making positive choices. Believe me, the decisions you make regarding the children will stay with you long after your children are grown. That's why I want you to start laying some positive groundwork—today.

Obviously, if you and your spouse had no children, the ramifications of getting divorced would be far less complicated. You could simply work out your property settlement and go your separate ways. If you so wished, the two of you would never even have to see each other again.

When there are children, however, this kind of clean break is virtually impossible. No matter how much you may despise each other, you and your spouse will have dealings for years to come, assuming that you both want to play a part in your children's lives. I realize that there is great irony in asking two people who could not collaborate successfully in their marriage to do so now that they are divorcing, but it is something all responsible parents must consider.

Cooperating with someone you perceive as an enemy is a tall order, but it is far from impossible. No matter how you feel about your estranged spouse, you have an obligation to make this parenting partnership work. Just remember, when it comes to doing the right thing by your children, it's what you *do* that counts—not how you feel.

You and your spouse have the opportunity to work out virtually any kind of custody and visitation arrangement you want. As time goes on, you will be able to restructure that arrangement in any way that is mutually acceptable. The courts in most states do not want to interfere with these decisions and will do so only in those cases in which two people cannot work things out for themselves.

In a sense, buzzwords like *custody* and *visitation* are irrelevant for couples who can work things out amicably. Nevertheless, the terms of your agreement pertaining to the children will be included in your divorce decree. As you negotiate, whether through attorneys or with a mediator, you will be doing so in the shadow of the law. Therefore, you may find it useful to understand the definitions and ramifications of some of the legal terms used in regard to children.

Exploring Some Basic Child-Care Concepts

Temporary physical custody. When a couple separates pending a divorce, one or the other will generally assume responsibility for the children. Temporary physical custody means that your children will live with you or your spouse until divorce proceedings are completed.

Separated couples often get into furious battles over temporary custody because they fear it will affect a judge's ultimate determination. In theory, this temporary determination is not supposed to influence the court's final decision. In practice, however, the parent with temporary custody is most likely to be favored.

Permanent custody. By the time your divorce is finalized, you will agree on (or the court will order) a permanent custody arrangement. Custody may be sole—that is, granted to one parent—or shared by both parents.

When one parent is awarded permanent custody, he or she is the one who is legally responsible for the children—even if they live with the other spouse 50 percent or more of the time. The custodial parent is the one who makes all decisions regarding a child's physical and emotional care, education, and religious training.

The term *physical custody* refers to the parent with whom the child resides. Generally speaking, the parent who receives sole physical custody will also have legal custody. In most *sole custody* situations, the noncustodial parent receives *visitation*.

In 1973, a well-known psychoanalyst–attorney team, which included the world-famous psychologist, Anna Freud, published a book called *Beyond the Best Interests of the Child*. This publication has greatly influenced the judicial philosophy behind many custody decisions.

The interdisciplinary author team found that the speed and permanence of the custody arrangements are more important than the issue of which parent is the more able custodian. They maintain that the interests of children of divorce are best served when one parent has complete control of custody. As for the other parent, the authors suggest that he or she have no enforceable right to see the child unless permission is granted by the custodial parent.

Freud and her colleagues strongly recommend *sole custody* as the arrangement that is most likely to maximize the emotional stability of a child's life. They contend that since most divorcing couples are too angry or hurt to cooperate in looking after the best interests of their children, a young person will fare better if he or she can bond to *either* the mother or father.

Courts in over thirty-five states, however, now prefer *joint custody* and other shared custody arrangements to those that tend to exclude one or the other parent. New York is part of a minority of states where *sole custody* is virtually the rule rather than the exception.

Whatever the benefits of *joint custody*, this is an arrangement that can work only if the two parents are able to cooperate with each other on an ongoing basis. Unfortunately, the custody cases that come to court are those in which the parties are most contentious and, therefore, least predisposed to cooperate.

Later in this chapter, we will examine the relative positions of mothers and fathers who find themselves embroiled in a custody battle. In theory, most states mandate that custody should be the awarded to the parent whose custodial care can serve the "best interests" of the child. While there are some differences between states, the most common criteria for what constitutes a child's best interests include:

- Relative stability of the environment each parent can provide.
- Emotional closeness or bonding with each parent.
- Physical health of each parent.
- Emotional fitness of each parent.
- Moral conduct of each parent.
- Ability and desire of each parent to provide ongoing care.
- Preference of the child (particularly with older children).
- Willingness to facilitate increased contact with the noncustodial parent (particularly in close cases).

As I've noted, the most bitter divorces are those that involve a protracted custody battle. This is the area of contention where world wars are most often waged—and on a variety of fronts.

Since a judge is obliged to base his or her decision on what is in the best interests of the child, the question of parental fitness often becomes a key issue. You can get into a whole series of fights and competing testimonies by expert witnesses, stating that one or the other parent is fit or unfit to care for the child. And, quite naturally, the other spouse will counter each expert with one of his or her own.

As a practical matter, you can generally find an expert to testify to just about anything. Ultimately, you wind up with a lot of contradictory testimony, enormous legal fees, and a growing hatred between the spouses.

One spouse often claims that the other spouse is unfit or unstable and that contact would be antithetical to the best interests of the child. Often this results in a series of *motions* for psychological or physical examination of either one or both spouses.

There are procedures by which either or both of the parties can make a motion before the court requesting psychological or physical examination of the other spouse to determine fitness for custody. The court may also direct that there be psychological or physical examination of the children as well.

As with any issue that is contended in court, you will have to go through the time-consuming legal process, including *discovery*, written *interrogatories*, oral testimony, and the rest. The worst of all, however, is your child being asked to testify on trial—a searing experience that is certain to exacerbate his or her pain.

Happily, most custody cases never reach this stage. In reality, there are many clear-cut cases that soon become self-evident to everyone involved. With rational lawyers, most spouses will eventually realize that going to war over custody and visitation is not going to help anyone—especially the children.

Look at it this way. Instead of spending thousands of dollars on extra legal fees, why not show your love for your child by placing that money in a savings account for his or her college education?

Experienced marital attorneys can usually anticipate the likely outcome of a custody case, should it go in front of a judge. With some couples, it is clear as to what is in the best interests of the child. Such cases generally can be resolved between the parties and their attorneys. On the other hand, there are some cases in which two fit parents both sincerely want sole physical custody. In such instances, a *shared custody* arrangement may be an appropriate solution—assuming the spouses are not bent on revenge and retribution.

Visitation

The relative benefits of *sole custody* versus *shared custody* arrangements are still vigorously debated, and I suspect the dissent will continue for many years to come. Even in cases in which one parent receives sole custody, judges now favor arrangements that allow both parents to be involved in their children's lives.

Through *visitation* rights, judges can achieve that objective by granting the noncustodial parent a reasonable amount of access to his or her children. Visitation rights typically include the right of the noncustodial parent to have the child stay overnight for short visits and holidays.

Since fewer than 10 percent of all divorcing couples go to court, we know that the vast majority of estranged parents resolve the issues of custody and visitation through their lawyers or by some collaborative process. In many instances, only one parent (typically the mother) truly wants sole physical custody of the children. The vast majority of fathers are satisfied with liberal visitation rights or a shared custody arrangement.

When it comes to visitation rights, many judges prefer not to spell out chapter and verse. They have learned through past experience that the specifics of visitation are difficult if not impossible to enforce if the parties are determined not to abide by the agreement.

Let's say a court-ordered visitation specifies that the child will stay at the noncustodial parent's house (in this case, the father) one weekend a month and be returned by six o'clock on Sunday. What is the mother to do if the father returns the child at nine o'clock? Call the police? Go back to court?

Judges are aware that such minor violations could potentially stifle an already overburdened court system. For that reason, they prefer granting the divorcing spouse a great deal of flexibility in working out the particulars of their arrangement. In any case, it is always a good idea to have the visitation agreement committed to writing. This is particularly important if your spouse has a proven record of unreliability or if you have reason to believe that he or she might not honor the agreement.

By having the terms of the visitation order spelled out, you will at least have an easier time establishing that your rights are being violated. And while going to court may not be a particularly desirable alternative, it is an option that you may be forced to exercise should all else fail.

Assuming that the resolution of child-care issues is not the result of a horrendous court battle, visitation is an area that is particularly well-suited to a collaborative and flexible approach. If you and your spouse can agree to cooperate for the sake of your child, you can alter the terms of visitation to suit your needs.

If there is some radical or negative change in circumstances, you can ask the court to modify visitation rights at any time. If, for example, your spouse has started abusing drugs or alcohol, you can ask that visitation be modified pending an investigation of such charges. If you can establish that there is extreme emotional instability, criminal activity, or physical or sexual abuse, you can ask the court to modify, curtail, or even terminate your spouse's visitation rights.

These may sound like drastic cases. Unfortunately, they are far from rare in modern society. If after consultation with your attorney and possibly a mental health professional, you honestly believe that your ex-spouse is posing a serious threat to your children, I suggest that you use every legal means at your disposal to terminate unsupervised visitation privileges. I must point out, though, that once charges of abuse are leveled, the case takes on a life of its own and cannot be side-tracked.

I feel certain that the vast majority of you are responsible people with genuine love and concern for your children. Therefore, if you end up becoming the noncustodial parent, a visitation arrangement that calls for contact on alternate weekends and major holidays may not seem like a particularly desirable arrangement. Even though you may not have wanted custody, you still don't want to feel that you are being shut out of your children's lives.

While I understand these feelings, I suggest that you subordinate them for your child's sake. Make the most of the time you have together. Let him or her know how very special those hours are to you. If the child responds well to your visitations and your ex-spouse is comfortable with the arrangement, the situation might change for the better. In time, your ex-spouse may come to acknowledge your value as a parent and encourage more involvement and contact on your part.

As the divorce trauma begins to recede, he or she may begin to regard you as a partner in ensuring your child's welfare, rather than as a bitter adversary. At that point, the two of you may consider increased visitation or even some kind of shared custody arrangement.

In any case, it is possible for noncustodial parents to play an important part in their children's lives. Ask your attorney to help you secure rights other than visitation as part of the divorce settlement. These can include educational, medical, and religious rights.

> **Educational:** The right to be informed by your child's school of his or her academic progress. The right to receive copies of report cards and meet with teachers in order to discuss your child's progress. The right to be informed of and to attend special school events. The right to participate in the selection of a special high school or college.

> **Medical:** The right to participate in major medical decisions. The right to review medical and dental records.

> **Religious:** The right to participate in decisions pertaining to where your child worships and receives religious training.

If you truly want to be an involved parent, I suggest that you attempt to obtain as many of these rights as possible. Once your divorce is finalized, try to follow through and make the most of your opportunities to participate in your child's upbringing. The so-called Disneyland Dad has become all too prevalent a phenomenon among noncustodial parents, and I strongly suggest that you avoid this role.

In case you are not familiar with the term, Disneyland Dad is a reference to parents (most often fathers) who use their visitation time as an opportunity to impress and entertain their children. Perhaps out of guilt stemming from the overall lack of contact, the parent attempts to compensate by showering the child with gifts and special events.

In a sense, this is a not-so-subtle form of propaganda, designed to convince the child of what he or she is missing by not living with the noncustodial parent. Of course, this is a distortion of reality. The custodial parent has the responsibility of the child's day-to-day care. Under the circumstances, it is impossible to create a party or holiday atmosphere on a continuing basis.

The noncustodial parent, on the other hand, often has a problem establishing and maintaining a genuine continuity in his relationship with the child. Therefore, it is understandable that he or she would attempt to compensate. Nevertheless, Disneyland Dads would be well-advised to temper these tendencies if they are primarily concerned with their children's long-range interests. Children appreciate gifts, but they are not likely to mistake treats for the genuine affection and concern they really need.

Mother vs. Father: Who Should Be Given Custody?

We have discussed some of the issues brought about by the shifting roles of men and women in our culture. To some extent, we all still are coping with these changing mores and expectations—both in ourselves and in terms of our roles as spouses and parents. Society as a whole, and the legal system in particular, cannot resolve these delicate issues nearly as well as two motivated people. And again, what can be a greater motivation than protecting the interests of your children?

It would be highly unrealistic to expect the legal system to take the lead in implementing sweeping social and interpersonal changes. Nevertheless, in recent years, family law statutes have started to reflect some of the radical turnabouts of the past few decades.

The whole notion of marriage as an economic partnership, for example, reflects a growing acknowledgment of the role women play in the family as well as in the workplace. As we've seen, however, there are aspects of this partnership concept that don't always work in a woman's favor. Let's examine this irony in terms of *child custody.*

Until recently, there was in most states a strong *maternal presumption* of who should have physical custody of the children. In other words, the mother was almost always awarded custody, barring some unusual circumstance.

Most states have now shifted to a *gender-neutral basis* for granting custody. In theory, this puts a father's claim as a child's custodial parent on an equal footing with the mother's. Nevertheless, the mother is still awarded custody in the overwhelming majority of divorce cases. Let's examine what is behind this.

One of the substantial factors the court takes into consideration in making a determination of custody is the question of who is and who has been the children's *primary caretaker.* Despite all the changes in the traditional concepts of mothering and fathering, it is still far more common for the husband to go to work and for the mother to stay home and take care of the children. Even in families in which both parents have full-time careers, it is more often the mother who takes the greater role in child-rearing.

Perhaps some of you might consider this an antiquated view of parental roles, just as it may be old-fashioned to take the position that the man is most often the monied spouse. In any case, it will take the legal system time to catch up to the social changes of the past few decades. There continues, however, to be an undeniable movement toward a true gender-neutral presumption.

As traditional mothering and fathering roles continue to evolve and intertwine, judges will no longer be able to use a fingertip-type test in making custody determinations. As more and more fathers can establish that they are indeed the children's primary caretakers, we will reach a point at which there is no longer even a de facto maternal presumption in the courts.

From year to year, I see definite progress being made in this area. Nevertheless, I think it is fair to say that, in the great majority of American homes, the mother is still the children's primary caretaker. Let's take a moment to examine this from a practical standpoint.

In the past, most middle-class Americans grew up in homes in which the father was out all day working, and the mother took care of the kids. If a child became sick, it was the mother who accompanied him or her to the doctor. If a parent was required to attend a P.T.A. meeting, it was the mother who went.

Today, many mothers choose to pursue full-time careers. Still, if a family decides that one parent should stay home and care for the children, it is most often the mother who will take on that role. Assuming that both parents are equally fit in most other respects, a judge will generally award custody to the parent who has spent the most time as the child's main caretaker. Let's consider some typical situations.

Up until the age of five, at which point a child starts attending school, he or she often stays at home with a nonworking mother. If such parents decide to divorce at this point, there is little question about who will receive custody.

One of the main concerns of the court in awarding custody is minimizing the disruption that divorce causes in a child's life. Thus, assuming the mother in our example is not a drug addict or totally off-the-wall emotionally, she will usually be awarded custody. Most judges would consider it antithetical to the best interests of the child to suddenly deem the father the primary caretaker—even though he may be totally qualified and appropriate for that role.

Now, let's assume that this same child is nine or ten, and attending school. The father is still working, and the mother has recently resumed her career. Unless the father can prove that he has taken over the role of primary caretaker, a judge is still likely to favor the mother, based on the bonding that has taken place throughout the child's life.

Remember, we're talking here in generalities. Even though the laws in most states now require a gender-neutral presumption, fathers who really want custody and are ready to fight it out in court must be prepared to counter existing predispositions and stereotypes.

Once the child reaches the middle- to late-teenage years, the father may be in a better negotiating position. At that point, a child is more peer-oriented than parent-oriented. School location and other logistic considerations may have more of an impact on a judge's decision. Also, a teenager's stated preference becomes a greater factor in the court's decision.

In recent years, there has been a great deal said and written about fathers' rights in regard to child custody. There is no doubt that most concerned fathers want ongoing access to their children and suffer great emotional pain when this is denied. Nevertheless, I find that, in a large percentage of cases, fathers really have no interest in assuming custody of the children—at least once they take a clear-eyed look at what this involves.

Let's take the case of George and Diane, who were seeking a divorce after ten years of marriage. George is thirty-five years old. Since graduating from college twelve years ago, he has worked as a civil engineer. Diane is thirty-three. She worked as a legal stenographer up until the birth of their first son, Ben, who is now eight. The couple's second son, Tom, is five. The husband was the moving party in this particular divorce.

When he first started working with his attorney, George had the notion that he wanted custody of the two boys. Let's listen in on part of a conversation between George and his lawyer:

> GEORGE. What are my chances of getting custody of the kids?
>
> ATTORNEY. Let's explore that for a little while. Why do you want custody? Are you interested in seeing them or having *physical custody* of them?
>
> GEORGE. I think I'd like physical custody, even though I've been told that this is usually awarded to the mother. Is it a given that my wife would prevail, assuming she had the same desire?
>
> ATTORNEY. That depends, in part, on how strongly you feel about this issue. How much are you willing to put on the line to back up the feeling—both in terms of dollars and emotions?

GEORGE. First tell me what the financial ramifications would be.

ATTORNEY. Would your wife be willing to go to the mat with you over the issue of custody?

GEORGE. I expect that she would.

ATTORNEY. Then we are probably talking about as much as another twenty-five thousand dollars in terms of the costs of the entire divorce proceeding, assuming the case goes to court. Remember, your wife is not working, so you are going to be the one footing the tab for virtually all the legal fees!

You also have another practical consideration. It is very easy to say that you want custody of the children, but it may turn out to be very difficult to actually have physical custody on a day-to-day basis. Let's look at that issue from a practical standpoint.

You have an eight-year-old and a five-year-old, both of whom get home from school at 3:00 P.M. What are the kids going to do between then and when you return from work at 7:00 P.M.? Unless you hire a housekeeper, it is going to be next to impossible to care for them properly.

GEORGE. Okay, I can see your point. Maybe she will be in a better position to handle those logistics. Maybe we should just drop the issue of physical custody and just go for liberal visitation. What do you think?

ATTORNEY. We don't necessarily have to drop it completely at this early juncture. Even if you decide that physical custody of your children isn't for you, it may be a good negotiating point to throw into the pot, at least for starters. Maybe down the line, you can give in on that in exchange for some concession on your wife's part.

Now, one could legitimately ask whether there is something wrong with using the issue of child custody to gain leverage in a negotiation. This is not an easy question for an attorney to answer.

I would always prefer that all issues pertaining to the children be resolved in as straightforward and cooperative a way as possible. In the real world, however, many lawyers have taken the same stance as George's attorney at one time or another. Still, there is a difference between raising an issue to establish a strong position during the opening rounds of a negotiation and using it as a battering ram in a protracted war.

Attorneys sometimes have an obligation to render advice that runs contrary to their adversarial bent. Although the line is far from clear, I believe that a concerned advocate is ethically bound to pressure clients to give priority to their children's welfare.

Ultimately, the primary obligation of parents is to their children, and I think it behooves an attorney to make that clear. Let me tell you just what I tell my clients.

"If you want to have an old-fashioned economic battle over the distributive award or alimony, go right ahead. It's your life and your choice. But if you approach questions pertaining to your children with swords in hand, you may do them irretrievable damage."

Shared Custody Arrangements

In a typical sole custody and visitation arrangement, one parent usually sacrifices a great deal of contact with the children. Of course, many of these situations work out perfectly well. Still, what happens when both parents want to continue playing a full and active role in their children's lives? For a growing number of divorced couples, the answer can be found in some kind of shared or joint physical custody arrangement.

Shared arrangements can make a great deal of sense because when they work they preserve a meaningful role for both parents in the child's postdivorce life. As with everything else, there are some definite problems with shared arrangements, and they are certainly not appropriate for every couple. Every couple should, however, seriously consider them. Many legal and mental health professionals now feel that, when circumstances are favorable, some kind of *shared custody* arrangement is most beneficial for the entire family.

More than thirty-five states have expressed a preference for shared custody arrangements because they enable both parents to maintain ongoing contact with the children. One kind of shared custody situation that has come into vogue is *joint custody*.

If you and your spouse can work it out, this can be a very positive arrangement for all concerned. In essence, joint physical custody means that the children continue to reside with both parents—albeit in two different homes. While such an arrangement has the advantage of facilitating the full participation of both parents, it can be financially expensive and logistically complicated. Nevertheless, if both parents reside close to each other, are committed to the arrangement, and can divorce their parental responsibilities from their dislike of their ex-spouses, a joint custody situation may best serve a child (and family's) long-term interests.

Great care must be taken in such arrangements to ensure continuity of the child's education and peer relations. A predictable and stable environment must be created so that a youngster does not feel like he or she is being constantly shuttled around from place to place. In the best joint custody arrangements, the child comes to feel as if this variety in his or her life is positive rather than an intrusion.

Lee and Barbara are one of an increasing number of divorced couples who have devised a satisfactory joint custody arrangement. Their ten-year-old son Arnold lives with each parent on alternate weeks. When the couple divorced four years ago, however, there was sufficient bitterness to make the likelihood of a shared custody arrangement seem highly doubtful.

Barbara had gotten pregnant one year after the marriage. When Arnold was five, she began to feel a great deal of dissatisfaction with the relationship. The couple went to marriage counseling for three months. At that point, Barbara decided that she and Lee were incompatible. Shortly thereafter, she filed for divorce.

Lee's initial response was one of rejection and disappointment. Nevertheless, he decided not to become embroiled in a bitter divorce battle—for the sake of the child. Basically, he was amenable to working out an equitable financial arrangement, but he became enraged when Barbara expressed a desire for sole physical custody.

Lee began attending individual counseling sessions. He was soon able to accept the termination of his marriage. On the other hand, he felt strongly about being deprived of contact with his son. Through his lawyer, Lee informed Barbara that he was ready to fight for his parental rights. Fortunately, both parties had reasonable attorneys, who arranged a *four-way conference* in hopes of resolving this matter.

Lee and Barbara both appeared to be stable individuals as well as devoted parents. Husband and wife were both working and neither planned to sacrifice their respective careers to become a full-time homemaker. Arnold was in school most of the day, and by the time he returned, both parents would be available to look after him.

Barbara's attorney felt convinced that Lee's parental desires were genuine. He even sensed that Lee might acquiesce in order to spare Arnold the distress of seeing his parents engaged in a bitter war. Nevertheless, Barbara's lawyer suggested that she and Lee enter into divorce counseling with the intention of hammering out some kind of mutually acceptable custody arrangement.

Husband and wife agreed to undergo divorce counseling. Within a few sessions, much of the initial bitterness began to dissipate. However, the couple was still far apart on the issue of custody.

When the possibility of *joint custody* arose, Lee had a favorable response. Barbara, on the other hand, absolutely hated the idea.

"No way," she angrily told the counselor. "I'm not going to split my son in half." At that point, Lee grew hostile. "I have no intention of letting you turn me into some kind of absentee father," he shouted.

As the sessions progressed, Barbara came to realize that a long-term custody situation that was unsatisfactory for Lee would be bound to make her and Arnold miserable. Eventually, she agreed to a joint physical custody arrangement that both spouses now consider successful.

Barbara continues to live in the three-bedroom townhouse she and Lee purchased five years earlier. Lee now lives in a spacious two-bedroom apartment three blocks away. Initially, it was agreed that Arnold would spend two weeks with each parent. But after three months of this arrangement, both parents felt that two weeks was too long a time away from their son. Both agreed to experiment with an alternate-week arrangement. This has proved satisfactory to all concerned.

Although neither of them has had a serious relationship since the marriage ended, Lee and Barbara both lead active social lives. The joint custody arrangement allows both parents the freedom to pursue their independent lives, and they have learned to make the most of this flexibility.

At one point, Barbara had to go on a three-week business trip. Lee was happy to take care of Arnold during that time. A few months later, Lee and a girlfriend wanted to vacation in Hawaii for two weeks. Barbara was pleased to take Arnold for an extra week.

Through cooperation and mutual respect, this family is able to make the most of joint custody. While Lee and Barbara don't consider themselves friends, they are cordial and considerate in making arrangements and living up to their responsibilities. When there are major decisions to be made or special occasions to attend, they feel comfortable about consulting each other and spending time together in their roles as concerned parents.

Arnold has always been close with both sets of grandparents. Because of his parent's amicable joint custody arrangement, the youngster is able to maintain these relationships pretty much as before. Even in more hostile arrangements, most courts acknowledge *grandparent's rights* in terms of maintaining ongoing contact with the child. However, as a practical matter, such rights are difficult to enforce if two estranged parents are determined to continue waging war.

Another kind of *shared custody* arrangement is *split custody,* which is structured so that one child resides with the mother, while the other resides with the father. Bob and Vivian divorced after twenty years of marriage. They had a seventeen-year-old son named Anthony and an eight-year-old daughter, Lorraine.

Upon their separation, Bob moved into an apartment about ten miles away from the family home. As it happened, Anthony planned to attend a community college that was within walking distance of Bob's new place. Also, father and son had a very close relationship. They regularly played tennis together and went on skiing trips in the winter.

Bob and Vivian agreed to hold onto their three-bedroom home until eight-year-old Lorraine was older. Both parents agreed that it would be disruptive to take her out of school and remove her from her familiar environment at this time. As much as possible, Bob tries to have Lorraine spend alternate weekends with him. On other weekends and holidays, Anthony stays with his mother and sister. Both parents have agreed that when Anthony moves out on his own, Vivian will have *sole custody* of Lorraine, while Bob will have *sole custody* of Anthony.

Limitations of Shared Custody Arrangements

If an outsider were to read about families who make joint and *split custody* work, he or she might wonder why such arrangements are not more prevalent. As I have noted, for shared custody to work, you must have two parents who can put their own feelings aside and cooperate in the child's best interests. It is obvious, therefore, that this kind of arrangement is not going to work out if two people are full of rage and hostility.

Another thing one has to look out for in *shared custody* arrangements is the rejected spouse who is using it as a last-ditch effort to hold onto the relationship. Not only is this kind of hidden agenda harmful to the parents, it can be disastrous for the children.

Mental health professionals have discovered that young people are more resilient in the face of divorce than was once thought. On the other hand, they require clear and consistent messages from both parents. A certain amount of friction and arguing can serve to reinforce that the parents are splitting up because they do not get along. But if one parent is using joint custody to maintain maximum contact with the other parent, this is bound to confuse the child and, perhaps, reinforce the feeling that the breakup is indeed the child's fault.

Some parents who seek shared custody do so to manipulate or vent hostility toward an ex-spouse. Such motivations may not be conscious, but this does not make them any less dangerous to you and your children. In assessing the suitability of you and your ex-spouse as good candidates for joint custody, you may want to ask yourself the following questions:

Is Joint Custody Right for Your Family?

1. Are you tempted to agree to joint custody simply to end the arguing, or do you honestly believe that it is a viable option?
2. In spite of the fact that the marriage didn't work out, do you honestly feel that your ex-spouse is a good parent?
3. Can you foresee cooperating with each other on an ongoing basis and avoiding manipulative games?
4. Are you confident that both of you will be able to share in making important decisions concerning your child's welfare?
5. If disagreements surface over *maintenance* or *child support,* will you be able to keep those issues separate from the ones that involve the child's emotional well-being?
6. If your ex-spouse remarries or becomes involved in a serious relationship, will you be able to accept that person as a potentially positive influence on your child rather than as a competitor?

I mentioned earlier that many states now advocate joint custody as the most desirable way to resolve child-care disputes. Some courts have even mandated such an arrangement as a compromise measure, even though neither parent really wanted it.

I strongly believe, however, that expedience is a terrible reason to opt for joint custody. Remember, if the arrangement turns out to be unsatisfactory, you might find yourself back in your attorneys' offices and even in court. Such an eventuality would prove highly disruptive to your children.

Some parents push for joint custody because they are sincerely afraid of being kept away from their children. In many cases, however, *sole custody* with liberal *visitation* for the noncustodial parent turns out to be the best solution. Again, if you and your ex-spouse are creative, flexible, and show respect for each other's rights, any arrangement can prove to be workable.

Ultimately, there is no one solution that is best for every family. However, the criteria for determining which option is best for you are exactly the same. In the end, you must ask yourself these two critical questions:

- Which possibility provides the children the freest and most comfortable access to both their parents?
- Which option provides the most continuity, while protecting the child's health and welfare?

No matter what solution you ultimately select, it is important that both of you feel involved and reasonably satisfied with the arrangement. It is very difficult for the court to enforce custody and visitation orders. Therefore, it is in everybody's best interests to forge an arrangement with which the whole family can live.

Whatever option you choose, I urge you to find a way to make these decisions in collaboration with your ex-spouse. Try to be creative and consider as many options as possible. If you will both try hard to keep the child's best interests in the forefront, I'm confident that you will find a solution that works for your family.

Guidelines for Protecting Your Children

Whenever I work with clients who are riddled with guilt because their divorce is disrupting their children's lives, I try to explain that it is not so much the divorce itself that is traumatic to children. The real damage is done when estranged parents continue fighting before, during, and long after the legal divorce is finalized. Certainly, all children of divorce are going to experience feelings of rejection and abandonment, but these can be minimized by two rational parents who make a sincere effort to handle the situation correctly.

Andrew Schepard, Esq., a professor of family law at Hofstra University, is a consultant to the New York State Law Revision Commission on child custody issues and a nationally known expert in this field. He makes the following observations:

"Divorce, in my view, is a major public health problem for children. A child's sense of order and stability can be shattered by the experience. Children view the day that one parent moves out as the most miserable day of their lives. School work suffers, as do relationships with friends and other adults. Some children have to grow up too fast in order to care for parents who are suffering from divorce-related problems. Divorce also seems to be associated with a long-term negative effect on the child's sense of optimism and the stability of male–female relationships.

"I am not saying that parents should stay in troubled marriages solely for the sake of their children. Some children do, in the long run, benefit from their parents' divorce because tension and turmoil in the family is reduced. The problem is that we do not know who these children are in advance.

"Above all, parents should avoid dragging their children into their battles. They should do what they can to avoid undermining the child's confidence in and relationship with the other parent. Whatever their problems with each other, parents should declare a demilitarized zone as far as their children are concerned."

As with everything else in life, there are appropriate and inappropriate ways of handling things. Please don't misunderstand: Nobody expects you to be perfect in this or any other matter. I just want you to start taking positive steps in terms of protecting your children. At the same time, I want to help you avoid the kinds of destructive mistakes untold numbers of separated and divorced parents have made—and are making at this very moment.

I thought it would be helpful to conclude our discussion with a summary of guidelines that attorneys and mental health professionals suggest in counseling clients. Again, nobody expects you be perfect. Still, if you find that you or your ex-spouse is having difficulty abiding by the commonsense principles, it might be a good idea to seek professional help.

Do's and Don't's for Divorced Parents

- Do make sure your children know (by specifically telling them) that you love them and that the divorce is not their fault.
- Don't have hostile, name-calling fights in front of the children.
- Do reassure your child that divorce is not a sign of personal failure or a cause for shame.
- Don't ask your child to choose whom he or she loves more or with whom he or she wants to live.
- Do establish positive patterns of child care from the beginning of the separation.
- Don't let your child feel like he or she is being shuttled between parents.
- Do let your child continue being a child.
- Don't use the child for emotional support or as someone in whom you confide your deep, dark secrets.
- Do encourage the child to have a continued relationship with your ex-spouse.
- Don't try to hurt your ex-spouse by discouraging visitation.
- Do try to establish and maintain a calm atmosphere and a stable environment.
- Don't say negative things about your ex-spouse—even if you feel strongly that they are true.
- Do try to establish and maintain regular patterns of visitation.
- Don't use your child to deliver messages (especially negative ones) to your ex-spouse.
- Do inform your child's teachers about your divorce and about any accompanying changes in living arrangements.
- Don't prevent your ex-spouse's parents and other relatives from having access to the child.
- Do try to include your spouse in important decisions and events in your child's life.

- Don't allow issues of visitation or custody to become linked with those of alimony and child support.
- Do continue to reassure your children that even though you and your spouse no longer love each other, you will always love and care for them.

A Final Word on Winning

I've often heard it said that nobody wins in a divorce—that the real issue is one of damage control. Perhaps on some very important level, this is true. Families and society would certainly be much better off if people took greater care in their choice of marriage partners and worked harder to resolve differences and problems within the marriage. Nevertheless, the prospects of some kind of global consciousness-raising are far more remote than those of winning at divorce.

If you are the one initiating the divorce, you are expressing an implicit hope of finding some light at the end of the tunnel— if not an outright victory. As a rejectee, on the other hand, it behooves you to turn a negative situation into one that is more positive.

While there are few if any clear-cut answers and easy solutions to complex problems, I do know many divorced men and women who can honestly say that, in the long run, the termination of their unsatisfactory marriage is the best thing that could have happened to them. On the other hand, there are some other divorced people who have never fully recovered from the trauma. Men and women in this latter category often are those who have undergone a bitter custody battle.

I know it may sound ironic, but if you are a divorcing parent, the most important key to winning may rest in putting someone else's needs before your own—those of your child. Remember, in order to really win at divorce, you must be able to move ahead in your life unencumbered by hatred, guilt, or the need for retribution.

There's no getting away from the fact that divorce is almost always a gut-wrenching experience, particularly if there are children involved. Nevertheless, the breakup of a marriage presents you with a very real opportunity to restructure your life and to make the kind of positive choices that will eventually lead to increased self-esteem.

If, somewhere down the road, you can look at your children and say: "I did what I could to love and protect them, even when it conflicted with my own selfish impulses," you will also be able to look at yourself without guilt.

Men and women who construct a positive self-image do so by overcoming adversity and acting responsibly. If you start with those building blocks—and supplement them with the knowledge and wisdom you have garnered from these pages—you will emerge a winner.

Glossary

ABANDONMENT   One of the grounds for separation or divorce. Abandonment generally requires proof of four elements: A) one spouse voluntarily separating; B) an intention not to return; C) lack of consent of the abandoned spouse to the separation; and D) no justification for the abandonment. The abandonment must exist for a year or more in order to be a basis for a divorce.

ADULTERY   One of the grounds for divorce. The commission of an act of sexual intercourse or deviant sexual intercourse voluntarily performed during marriage by the defendant with a person other than the spouse.

ALIMONY   See **maintenance.**

ANTENUPTIAL AGREEMENT   See **postnuptial agreement.**

ARBITRATION   Similar to a judicial determination in that the parties, in an informal atmosphere, authorize a neutral third party to make a binding resolution on various issues.

BILL OF PARTICULARS   A document obtained by serving a "demand" requesting the particulars or specifics of the opposing party's case. It sets forth details about the allegations in the pleadings, is used to limit the scope of the proof, and also prevents surprises from occurring at the trial.

BURDEN OF PROOF   The duty of affirmatively proving facts in dispute on an issue in the lawsuit.

CHILD CUSTODY   See **joint custody, shared custody,** and **split custody.**

CHILD SUPPORT   Funds paid by one or both parents to provide for the reasonable living and educational needs of the child.

COMMUNITY PROPERTY STATES   A state in which all property acquired during the marriage is deemed, upon divorce, to be divided equally between the spouses.

COMPLAINT   The first pleading in a lawsuit. The complaint sets forth the plaintiff's claims against the defendant on which the plaintiff seeks affirmative relief from the court. The facts set forth by the plaintiff must be sufficient to permit the plaintiff to obtain relief under a specific theory of the case, e.g., abandonment, adultery, etc. The subsequent pleadings are an answer and/or a counterclaim by the defendant and a reply by the plaintiff to the counterclaim. The answer and the reply admit or deny the claims set forth in the complaint or the counterclaim.

CONFERENCE JUDGE   The judge to whom a case is assigned.

CONSTRUCTIVE ABANDONMENT   This is a basis for separation or divorce. It may be sexual abandonment or refusal by one spouse to permit the other spouse to reenter the marital home. See **abandonment.**

CONVERSION DIVORCE   The parties must have lived separate and apart for one or more years, pursuant either to a **separation agreement** or **judgment of separation,** and the plaintiff proves that he or she has substantially performed all of the terms and conditions of the **decree** or agreement.

COUNTERCLAIM   A cause of action by a defendant against the plaintiff. See **complaint.**

COURT REPORTER   The person who transcribes testimony taken at a trial or at an examination before trial.

CRUEL AND INHUMAN TREATMENT   One of the grounds for separation or divorce. Conduct by the defendant that so endangers the physical or mental well-being of the plaintiff as to render it unsafe or improper for the plaintiff to continue to live with the defendant.

DECREE   See **judgment.**

DEFENDANT   The party being sued.

DEPOSITION   See **examination before trial.**

DISBURSEMENTS   Monies paid out of pocket to the court or to a third party (expert, process server, court reporter, etc.) during a lawsuit.

DISCOVERY   The group of procedures available after the action has been started which are used to obtain evidence and information relevant to, or material and necessary to, the lawsuit. The *discovery* procedures provide a means to: A) obtain testimony, admissions, and evidence to assist in proving your own case; and B) obtain information regarding your adversary's case. The procedures permit you to avoid surprise and gather your responsive proof. Discovery devices include depositions (examinations before trial); examination and copying of books, papers, and other things (discovery and inspection); written interrogations; physical and/or psychological examination; demands for admissions, etc.

DIVORCE DECREE   See **judgment.**

DOCKETING   The process by which a clerk of the court enters a judgment as an official record of the court.

EQUITABLE DISTRIBUTION   A process broadly defined to encompass a concept of property distribution under which all property acquired by either spouse during the course of the marriage—regardless of the type of property, or who holds title to same, or where it is located—is distributed "equitably" (read as fairly) between the spouses on divorce.

EXAMINATION BEFORE TRIAL Sworn, out-of-court testimony obtained from a party or a witness to obtain facts or opinions relevant or material and necessary to the lawsuit. A discovery device in which the testimony of either a party or a witness is taken, under oath before a court reporter. The testimony is reduced to writing (transcribed), and reviewed and sworn to by the witness.

EXPERT WITNESS FEES Fees paid to an accountant, actuary, appraiser, physician, psychiatrist, etc., in connection with the services they render to investigate, evaluate, appraise, or testify in the lawsuit.

FAULT STATES Those states in which it is necessary to prove that one of the spouses engaged in conduct satisfying the statutory grounds for divorce, e.g., adultery or abandonment for one or more years.

FOUR-WAY CONFERENCE A conference attended by the parties and their attorneys.

GENDER-NEUTRAL BASIS The basis upon which laws are applied without regard to the gender of either of the parties.

GRANDPARENT'S RIGHTS The privilege conferred by law that permits grandparents, in the discretion of the court, to compel a reluctant parent to grant visitation with a grandchild.

INCARCERATION Being in jail.

INTERIM COUNSEL FEES Legal fees awarded by the court to be paid by the other spouse during the pendency of a lawsuit.

INTERROGATORIES Written questions to be answered by the opposing party. See **discovery.**

JOINT LEGAL CUSTODY (ALSO KNOWN AS **SHARED CUSTODY**) Involves an agreement or court order under which both parents share physical possession of the child and each has equal voice in child-raising responsibilities, including decisions affecting the health, education, and welfare of the child. Over thirty states have statutes that permit joint custody.

JOINT PROPERTY Real or personal property, title to which is legally held in the name of husband and wife.

JUDGMENT It is the object of the lawsuit to obtain a judgment (sometimes called a decree) from the court determining the rights of the parties involved in the divorce.

MAINTENANCE Monies paid by one spouse pursuant to agreement or court order for the living expenses and/or reasonable needs of the recipient spouse.

MARITAL PROPERTY   In essence, all property acquired jointly or by
either spouse during the marriage. Not all states agree however on
what constitutes marital property. In some states, property acquired by one spouse before marriage remains separate property,
while in other states it is classed as marital property. States vary on
whether gifts from one spouse to the other are included as marital
property.

MARTINDALE-HUBBELL   A comprehensive series of books published by
Martindale-Hubbell Publishing that contains material about attorneys and law firms throughout the United States. Often this includes personal and professional biographical material concerning
the attorneys.

MATERNAL PRESUMPTION (ALSO KNOWN AS **TENDER YEARS DOCTRINE**)   A
doctrine whereby a court will favor the granting of custody of a
young child to his or her mother. The theory behind it was that
a mother was a more "fit" parent for a child up to the age of ten
or twelve years.

MEDIATION   A nontherapeutic process by which the parties, together
with the assistance of a neutral resource person, attempt to system-
atically isolate points of agreement and disagreement. They seek
to explore alternatives and consider compromises or accommoda-
tions so as to reach a consensual settlement on economic, custody,
and/or visitation issues relating to their divorce. It is an alternative
method of conflict resolution.

MEMORANDUM OF UNDERSTANDING   A writing prepared by the mediator
outlining the partners' agreements about the results of the mediation process. This forms the basis for the attorney to prepare the
separation agreement.

MODIFICATION OF CUSTODY   A change in a custody arrangement due to
facts that have arisen after the initial custody agreement or order.

MOTION PRACTICE   Once a lawsuit has been commenced, one of the
parties may wish to obtain some preliminary relief from the court.
The relief is requested by means of an application for a court order—this is called a motion. There are many types of motions that
may be made either before or during the trial. Motions are generally made in writing. Motions before trial may include a motion for
a preliminary injunction; a motion for a protective order to prevent
harassment of a party; a motion for temporary maintenance, child
support, custody, or use for the marital home; a motion for a temporary order of protection of the safety of one of the litigants; or
discovery motions. Motions during the trial may include a request
to strike a witness's answer as not being responsive, etc.

MOTIONS   See **motion practice.**

NET-WORTH STATEMENT   A document written under oath containing information regarding each party's living expenses, income, assets (real and personal), and liabilities. The truth of the contents of the statement is sworn to before a notary public.

NO-FAULT DIVORCE   A party need not prove that his or her spouse is at fault. The divorce is based on a no-fault allegation that there are irreconcilable differences between the spouses, or that there has been an irretrievable breakdown of the marriage, or that the spouses are incompatible, or have lived separately for a required period of time. As of 1990, thirty-six states permit no-fault divorce on the grounds of irreconcilable differences or irretrievable breakdown of the marriage.

NON-ABANDONMENT LETTER   A document in which one spouse agrees that he or she will not consider the other spouse's moving from the marital home an abandonment, which would form the basis for the remaining spouse's obtaining a divorce.

NOTE OF ISSUE   A case is placed on the trial calendar by serving and filing a note of issue. This is otherwise known as a *notice of trial.* Generally, a note of issue contains information about the case, including the names and addresses of the attorneys, the dates when the summons and the answer were served, whether a jury trial is being demanded, the nature and object of the action, and the fact that all discovery proceedings have been completed and the case is in all respects ready for trial.

NOTICE OF APPEARANCE   A written notice that the defendant appears in the lawsuit. The notice requests that a copy of the complaint and of all other papers in the action be served upon the individual serving the notice of appearance. It is used when a summons without a complaint accompanying it is served.

NOTICE OF TRIAL   See **note of issue.**

NOTICES OF DISCOVERY AND INSPECTION   This is a "disclosure device." The notices of discovery and inspection permit the party seeking discovery to inspect, copy, test, or photograph (or photostat) any specifically designated document that is in the possession, custody, or control of the other party. It is available against parties to the action as well as nonparty witnesses. See **discovery.**

ORDER OF EXCLUSIVE OCCUPANCY   An order of the court granting sole occupancy of the marital residence to one spouse and excluding the other spouse from residing in the residence or entering into same for any other purposes.

ORDER OF PROTECTION   An order of the court setting forth reasonable conditions of behavior to be observed for a specified period of time by either of the parties to the litigation. An order of protection may require one of the parties to stay away from the home, the other spouse, or the child; to abstain from offensive conduct against the child or against the other parent; to give proper attention to the care of the home; to refrain from acts of commission or omission that tend to make the home not a proper place for the child; to participate in an educational program; and to provide either directly or indirectly by means of medical and health insurance for expenses incurred for medical care and treatment arising from the incident or incidents that form the basis for the issuance of the order.

PARALEGAL   A lawyer's assistant who is not an attorney.

PENDENTE LITE   Orders issued pendente lite are orders issued by the court during the pendency of the litigation.

PLAINTIFF   The party who started the lawsuit.

PLEADINGS   Documents in a lawsuit in which the parties set forth the facts constituting their claims and defenses. The basic pleadings in a lawsuit are the complaint, the answer, the counterclaim, and the reply to the counterclaim.

POSTNUPTIAL AGREEMENT   An agreement entered into by a husband and wife subsequent to their marriage, defining their rights and obligations in the event of a divorce or death. See also **prenuptial agreement.**

PRENUPTIAL AGREEMENT   An agreement entered into by the prospective husband and wife prior to their marriage, defining their rights and obligations in the event of a divorce. It usually covers such issues as property division in the event of divorce or death and maintenance/alimony. It may also cover such issues as custody (a court is not bound by the parties' agreement), child support, and visitation.

PRIMARY CARETAKER   Professor Clark in THE LAW OF DOMESTIC RELATIONS IN THE UNITED STATES, Sec. 20.4, Pp. 449–501 (1987) defines the term as follows: "Primary caretaker is . . . the parent who has had the primary responsibility for the day-to-day and hour-to-hour care of the child, who has fed him, clothed him, arranged for his medical care, taken him to and from school, taught him in the home and been responsible for his discipline."

QUANTUM OF PROOF   The amount of proof necessary to sustain a party's burden of proof. See also **burden of proof.**

REHABILITATIVE MAINTENANCE   An amount of support/maintenance/

alimony awarded to one of the spouses for a limited period of time to enable that spouse to become self-supporting.

RELIEF   An order or judgment of the court granting certain assistance or rights to the plaintiff or defendant.

RETAINER   An agreement under which a party engages or employs the services of a lawyer or another professional.

SEPARATE PROPERTY (SEE **MARITAL PROPERTY**)   Generally, property held by one spouse prior to marriage, inherited property and gifts from one spouse to the other.

SEPARATION AGREEMENT   An agreement entered into by the husband and wife, stating that the parties have or will separate and settling the issues of property division, maintenance, custody, estate rights, child support, visitation, etc.

SHARED CUSTODY   See **joint legal custody.**

SOLE CUSTODY   One parent is vested, temporarily or permanently, by agreement or court order, with legal custody of a child under eighteen years of age and is responsible for the care, upbringing, and education of the child as well as for all decisions pertaining to the child's welfare.

SPLIT CUSTODY   Involves more than one child. Each parent has physical custody of one child.

SPOUSAL SUPPORT   See **maintenance.**

SUBORN PERJURY   The crime of permitting another person to testify falsely under oath.

SUMMARY DISSOLUTION LAW   See **no fault divorce**.

SUMMONS   The document by which a lawsuit is commenced upon its service on the defendant or filing with the clerk of the court.

SUNSET PROVISION   A provision in a document that automatically terminates the legal effect of that document at the conclusion of a given period of years.

TEMPORARY ORDERS (PENDENTE LITE)   Direction or decision issued by a court during the pendency of an action, which may affect custody, child support, maintenance, or other issues.

Bibliography

American Academy of Matrimonial Lawyers. *Certified Fellows*. Chicago, IL: AAML, 1990.

American Bar Association. *Directory of Litigation Attorneys*. Englewood Cliffs, NJ: Prentice-Hall, 1989.

Belli, Melvin and Mel Krantzler. *Divorcing*. New York: St. Martin's Press, 1988.

Block, Julian. *Julian Block's Year-Round Tax Strategies*. Rocklin, CA: Prima Publishing and Communications, 1990.

Fisher, Roger and William Ury. *Getting To Yes: Negotiating Agreement without Giving In*. New York: Penguin, 1983.

Franks, Maurice R. *Winning Custody*. Englewood Cliffs, N.J.: Prentice-Hall, 1983.

Freud, Anna, Joseph Goldstein, and A.J. Solnit. *Beyond the Best Interests of the Child*. New York: Free Press, 1983.

Gardner, Richard A. *The Boys' and Girls' Book About Divorce*. New York: Bantam, 1970.

Goleman, Daniel. "Two Views of Marriage Explored," *New York Times* (April 1, 1986), Section C, Science Times, Page 1.

Hodges, William F. *Interventions for Children of Divorce*. New York: Wiley-Interscience, 1986.

Katz, Sanford N., (ed.). *Negotiating to Settlement in Divorce*. Clifton, N.J.: Prentice-Hall Law and Business, 1987.

Kalter, Neil. *Growing Up with Divorce*. New York: Free Press, 1990.

Lansky, Vicki. *Divorce Handbook for Parents*. New York: NAL Books, 1989.

Martindale-Hubbell Legal Directory. New Providence, NJ: Martindale-Hubbell, Inc., 1990.

Medved, Diane. *The Case Against Divorce*. New York: Donald I. Fine, Inc., 1989.

Ware, Ciji. *Sharing Parenthood After Divorce*. New York: Viking Press, 1982.

Wallerstein, Judith S., and Sandra Blakeslee, *Second Chances: Men, Women and Children A Decade After Divorce*. New York: Ticknor and Fields, 1989.

Weitzman, Lenore J. *The Divorce Revolution*. New York: Free Press, 1985.

Who's Who in American Law. Wilmett, IL: Macmillan Directory Division, 1990–1991.

Index

About the Author

BERNARD ROTHMAN, J.D., practices law in New York. Mr. Rothman is a Graduate of New York University School of Law and is a former Assistant United States Attorney and former Acting Village Justice. The author is a Fellow of the American Academy of Matrimonial Lawyers, a member of the Executive Committee of the New York State Bar Association's Family Law Section, and co-chair of the Interdisciplinary Forum of Mental Health and Family Law. Mr. Rothman has been published in *The Family Law Review* and the *New York State Bar Journal* and has been quoted in the national press. He is a frequent lecturer to legal and mental health organizations. He is listed in *Who's Who in American Law, Who's Who in the East,* and *Who's Who in the World.* He is a partner in the New York City law firm of Finkelstein Bruckman Wohl Most & Rothman. Attorney Rothman makes his home in Westchester County, New York.